Bee
l g

Tips and Technologies

by David Kerrigan

Preface

I've just delivered the loneliest presentation I've ever given, even though it was to over 2,500 people. Thanks to the strange online-only world many of us have been in since early 2020, I had to address an invisible global audience from my spare room, seemingly talking to myself about "the Future of Retail", instead of presenting to a live audience.

It's remarkable that this is even possible, let alone that it needs little special equipment. I hope the advice in this book, based on my own experiences of presenting online to large and small audiences, and observing numerous webinars, helps more people reach their audience in the most impactful way possible, while staying safe.

Acronyms & Abbreviations

DSLR	Digital Single Lens Reflex - a type of camera, with interchangeable lenses.
FPS	Frames per Second - number of images that make up a video feed
FOV	Field of View - width of area visible to camera
HD	High Definition - image resolution of 720p or 1080p (Full HD) or 4K (Ultra HD)
HDMI	Type of connector for video/TV/monitors. Note some cameras use Mini or Micro HDMI connectors.
HVAC	Heating, Ventilation and Air Conditioning
Lav	Lavalier - a small clip-on microphone
MCU	Medium Close Up - camera framing that shows a person approximately from the mid-chest up
MS	Medium Shot - camera framing that shows a person approximately from the waist up
OBS	Open Broadcaster Studio - free software for advanced video recording and streaming controls
SPL	Sound Pressure Level - maximum sound level a microphone can handle before it distorts, measured in decibels
TRS	Tip Ring Sleeve - a type of 3.5mm connector
TRRS	Tip Ring Ring Sleeve - a type of 3.5mm connector
USB	Universal Serial Bus - a type of connector for computers
XLR	Type of connector commonly used for microphones

Contents

Chapter 1: Introduction

More online presentations were delivered in 2020 than in all previous history. Unfortunately, more *bad* online presentations have also been delivered in 2020 than in all previous history. Adapting to widespread working from home has forced us to dive into new ways of working, with little opportunity for preparation and, rightly, people have been focused on surviving the challenge as best they can. But as we search for the best ways to cope, for frequent presenters it's worth spending some extra time looking at the simple techniques to make online talks and webinars more impactful, rather than failing to adapt and thus disappointing their audiences.

Presenting online is undoubtedly different than presenting in person and for many people, initially more difficult. It's definitely harder to present without live audience feedback, without that certainty of being in the same room with people, knowing what they are experiencing and seeing how they're responding. It's daunting to navigate technological challenges without an IT or AV team for support, and it's also challenging to adapt your material to better suit fully-digital delivery.

Getting setup for virtual presenting will take some time upfront - an investment that is well worthwhile - but as soon as possible, you want to devote most of your energy to the content of your presentation rather than the broadcasting setup. By the end of this book, I hope to have helped you optimise your surroundings; identify if you need any additional hardware; and given you the confidence to deliver outstanding online presentations.

Rightsizing: From Pragmatic to Professional

This book is intended to help presenters used to delivering speeches, pitches or lectures in boardrooms, classrooms and auditoria who now find themselves in unfamiliar territory, facing a camera instead of an audience. Although the tips in this guide may help you look better prepared for any online meeting, it's primarily relevant in 'one-to-many' presentation situations or for formal client pitches as well as interviews, and not necessarily applicable to regular team meetings or family quiz nights!

To help you stand out from the crowd and deliver the very best online presentations possible, this book takes you through the easy basic improvements as well as some of the more costly ones, right up to tips for aspiring professionals.

Everyone's situation and requirements will be different, so I've included three broad categories along a continuum of possible solutions - a low or zero budget option for pragmatists, a more involved and expensive upgrade option for those seeking a more polished look, and examples of premium solutions for those looking to achieve more professional results. Feel free to mix and match from each category to meet your specific needs - for example you may need to overcompensate on the sound-related advice if you live in an echoey or basically noisy location, even if I would otherwise recommend those products only for professional-level presenters.

Pragmatic Presenters

I would expect the majority of people to fall into this category, where presenting isn't a primary job role but you may still need, on occasion, to present to colleagues or clients. Your efforts to make the most of your situation, without requiring major investment of time or money, will reflect positively on how you are perceived and on your credibility.

Polished Presenters

For those who are expected to give fairly regular, medium-scale presentations, lectures or guest appearances at conferences, I'd recommend a mixture of strategic investments in some key technologies and careful efforts to improve your skills, as well as a little more focus on your environment.

Professional Presenters

For presenters of large-scale presentations to prestige events, it may be desirable or even necessary to invest in multiple technology aids and invest additional time to hone your skills for the new online world. But even this level of commitment to presenting excellence is, thankfully, achievable and affordable.

'Horses for Courses'

I'm very mindful as I compile this guide, that those reading it will be at very varying points in their needs, surroundings, budgets and constraints. So in trying to present a continuum of solutions, I hope to help address as many combinations and permutations as possible but, ultimately, it's your choice as to what's appropriate - from a need and/or a budget point of view. Even the suggestions I make that are cost-free may be impractical in your situation and, while I obviously believe improving the quality of presentations is a worthy goal, you probably don't want to turn your home into a studio and permanently shred the boundaries of your work-life balance that's already under threat.

Depending on how frequently you find yourself presenting and on the scale of your audience, I hope this book can help you make relevant, proportionate choices; of course, it's absolutely legitimate to conclude that sections aren't necessarily relevant for your needs. What I want to ensure is that you make explicit choices and don't sell yourself short through a lack of awareness. But do give consideration to what you want to achieve from your presentations and seek external feedback - some of these optimisations are subtle, subconscious and even marginal in nature, but often impossible to judge without an audience. I've watched presenters carry on in blissful ignorance as they are shaking their camera by knocking their desk, moving a mouse on their desk that broadcasts as noisily as nails on a chalkboard or sharing slides that don't quite fit on the screen; it's hard to be self-aware with no feedback and a hesitancy on the part of an audience to point out flaws, for fear it's evident at their end only.

If you only give the occasional presentation, it may be harder to justify any investment in additional hardware or software. In many cases, the more you try to improve, you may reach a point of diminishing or even negative returns. The added complexity may distract from the content or have unintended consequences. Achieving the final few percentage point improvements may require expertise that you don't have and things like trying to hide cables can ultimately offset the intended improvements - for example, hiding a clip-on mic[1] can lead to rubbing against clothing, creating

---

[1] While some people opt for an abbreviation of 'mike' for microphone, I prefer mic. Both are acceptable, though the AP Stylebook and, more importantly, my spell checker, use mic

noise that negates the gains from improved proximity to the speaker's mouth.

The New Presenting

Presenting online is suddenly a key new career skill for many people, either as an extension of your current skill set or perhaps a fresh chance to add it as a new ability. Whether you're an experienced presenter or someone who has been hesitant about public speaking, online webinars and conferences represent a new way of doing things. Even the most polished, seasoned presenter needs to consider adaptations to their style, techniques or technologies to make the most of the new world. While content is still king, engaging with your audience via online presenting brings its own specific challenges.

The two biggest changes are the lack of a physically present audience, and the mediation of layers of technology. Adjusting to these two aspects requires presenters to revamp their content, alter their delivery and learn about new technologies. The good news is that, with a few adjustments and minimal investment, you can quickly set yourself apart from those who don't lean into the new realities.

The Invisible Audience

One of the many learnings of 2020 has been about what we took for granted - most presenters never really thought about the benefits of having a live audience co-located with them. But when you lose the ability to "read the room", a vital intangible indicator that strongly influences a good presentation is gone. As a presenter, you no longer have a sense of how your material is landing, without an audience to engage with, it really does feel like you're talking to yourself.

Even if you can't see participants, the audience is still the key focus of any presentation. The most important starting point for online presenting is to be mindful of how people are consuming your content - gone is the forced attention, the homogeneity of experience and, most importantly, the immediacy, the feedback, the sense of how it's being received in real time. The chance to gauge the audience is gone or greatly diminished but mustn't be forgotten.

Dedicated Facilities

Alongside the lack of a visible audience, the second key change is the lack of a dedicated, well-resourced presentation space. When presenting physically on a large stage, you expect the venue to provide suitable amplification and microphone(s), a big screen and AV staff to quickly remedy any technical hitches and glitches. When forced to present from your home, the carefully designed auditorium with the expensive AV technology is no longer there as a welcoming stage for your pronouncements and it's up to you to improvise and adapt.

At home, you should ensure, as far as possible, that you have both the 'stage' and the equipment suited to the task. You may not have a spot lit podium surrounded by acoustic panelling but, as we'll see in later chapters, there is still a lot you can do to find and improve even temporary spaces in your home. We perhaps shouldn't be surprised that the integrated equipment in a laptop designed for general computing - not online presenting - doesn't feature the optimum components and may require supplemental purchases, or, at the very least, amendments to how we approach it.

The New Presenters?

As a regular presenter who enjoys speaking to large audiences, it always saddens me when people struggle with public speaking. Looking for positives among the disruptions of 2020, a lot of the reasons that hold people back from public speaking are now gone. In fact, for some people who don't like it, the new world may be a significant opportunity to raise their profile on a virtual stage, without the fears associated with the physical stage.

Though obviously not without its innate challenges, presenting to a virtual audience offers a lot more forgiveness than being in front of a physical one. The virtual presenter, away from the full visibility of the attendees, can arrange their environment to provide any supports they need. Just out of shot of your webcam, you can now have notes and reminders that you wouldn't have on stage. Tend to get a bit hot and bothered if you're asked to present? Now you can arrange a (silent!) fan to help you keep your cool without anyone knowing. Unlike a live venue that you might not see until moments before you go on stage, you can practice in the exact conditions you'll have for delivering the real event. You can choose and use your own equipment - I've lost count of the number of times I've been handed a clicker that was far more cumbersome than my own, microphones that didn't fit well or been offered ancient (VGA) cables to connect to my laptop that only supports the more modern HDMI cables without an adaptor. If you're a nervous presenter, these little variations can disturb your rhythm.

I really hope that hesitant presenters can gain some additional confidence and advance their careers by practicing and learning the skills of presenting online without the added pressure of a visible audience.

Technology to the Rescue

Without technology, it would undoubtedly have been much harder to continue business and education activities during lockdowns and periods of restricted travel. Platforms like Zoom, Google Meet and Microsoft Teams have risen to the challenge of keeping the world connected, and although most people look forward to resumption of in-person events, there seems little doubt that online will remain the preferred channel in some cases, long after the pandemic has passed.

I will argue that content remains king whether a presentation is online or at a physical event, but the appropriate use of technology is a huge factor in how well or poorly an online presentation comes across. Knowing which technologies to use and when can distinguish the professional and engaging from the amateur and unprepared. It adds immensely to your credibility if you seem in control of the technology and have taken the time to ensure you come across well. It may be subtle - few in the audience will actually be thinking "that's a well-lit, well-framed presenter" - but subconsciously, getting the basics right enhances your credibility.

Broadcast Expectations

When we watch an online presentation our frame of reference is that of watching TV. Unlike our expectations when in a team meeting or on a social video call - both scenarios where poor audio and video quality are more tolerated - when attending a webinar or professional presentation, we have much higher expectations - expectations that often exceed the capabilities of the default setup, consisting of a laptop webcam and integrated microphone being used without due regard to lighting and framing, as we'll discuss in the coming chapters.

As much of the world moved into remote working from March 2020, there was a very obvious and sustained surge of Google searches for Webcams and Microphones as the shortcomings of the technology available to most people quickly became clear.

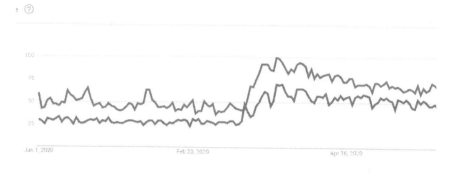

Figure 1: Google Trends searches in early 2020 for Webcam (top) and Microphones (bottom)

Unintended Markets/Thanks to the Gamers

Luckily, the range and affordability of higher quality AV technology have never been better. As we'll see throughout the second part of this book, an incredible array of technology exists that brings broadcast quality within reach of domestic budget users.

Technology developed for, and marketed to, bloggers and gamers, YouTube stars and influencers means prosumer[2] gadgets were available to be repurposed for business use. These devices came to exist because of the rise of streaming, social media and podcasts, but they are also ideal for business presenters looking to enhance their capabilities. If you're not familiar with the worlds of online streaming and podcasting, the relevant point is that their proponents have harnessed lighting, microphone and video technologies to produce studio-quality outputs on amateur budgets.

---

[2] Professional Consumer

Paying for It

As I explore ways to improve online presentation quality, I'm amazed at how many of the more impactful improvements require little expenditure. With no or negligible extra spending, I hope most readers will be able to improve their surroundings, lighting and framing. Everyone should be able to improve their content for free, aided if necessary by the software coaching tools discussed in chapter 9.

For others, improvements may be as simple as investing in a few extension cables rather than expensive hardware - being able to elevate your laptop or move to another side of the room that's further away from a power socket but offers better lighting may be all you need. I'll also highlight opportunities to repurpose devices you may already have or can borrow - someone you know may well have an excellent DSLR camera that they won't be taking on holidays anytime soon and can give it to you (via contactless delivery of course).

Going Further

After you've read this book, if you do identify the need to spend some money on improved hardware, it may be worth asking your boss if your employer is willing to cover or contribute to the costs. Many employers - for example Shopify[3] - have been willing to invest in technology to help their staff be more comfortable and productive when working from home. If you're self-employed, ask your financial adviser if any of your expenses are tax deductible.

For professional speakers, it's likely easier to justify investing - it becomes about production as well as presentation if you are a regular presenter at events where attention to detail and best practice are expected - those that take it seriously need more serious tools. If you had given 20 talks in a normal year, isn't it safe to say you'd have spent £50 per time on taxis to and from the venue? If so, a budget of £1,000 makes sense to ensure that your online presentations, from home where you've no travel expenses, are top quality.

---

[3]https://www.cnbc.com/2020/03/12/coronavirus-shopify-gives-employees-1000-stipend-to-work-from-home.html

Ready....Set....Zoom!

Inevitably, change as dramatic as the large scale move to online events requires a bit of a reset - but once you've made a few decisions and practiced, you can get back to focus fully on delivery, having mastered the tools and technologies. Although online is a new medium for many presenters, requiring different tools and different skills, there is an opportunity for both experienced and new presenters to shine.

If it feels like I'm stating the obvious at any point, that's great - it means you're already well in control and attuned to the topic. if you get just one additional tip out of this material that improves your audiences' experiences, then it's worthwhile reading the stuff you already know as a reminder.

Although I'll spend the majority of this book talking about techniques and technologies you'll need to consider for excellent online presenting, I want to start with an emphasis on the fundamentals of good presentations - your preparation as a presenter, as well as your content and its suitability for your audience. Then we'll talk about your environment, before delving into the technology that will enable you to shine.

Many of the individual topics here are worthy of their own book - when I studied broadcasting and video production in college, we had copious texts on each of the skills of lighting, sound design or video composition. However, my goal here is not to turn you into a broadcasting or technology expert; it is to set you up for success as an online presenter with pragmatic tips to free you from worrying about the new mechanics.

People will generally be more forgiving given the new circumstances, perhaps empathetic with, or amused by, difficult domestic conditions. But there's still a lot of competition out there and standards are improving as people get over the initial shock and settle in to the realisation that regardless of vaccines and therapeutics, there will be a lot more online presenting in the future than we were used to. Read on to see how to make the most of it in your circumstances.

Chapter 2: Content

Delivering your presentation while standing at the top of a room is no longer feasible in many professional and educational situations. Amidst the change, though, there are some constants - the quality of the content remains crucial, and polished delivery by a good presenter is essential to keeping the audience engaged. Irrespective of the medium, impactful presentations are engaging, well-structured, succinct and informative or persuasive. Effective presenters are prepared, poised, professional and have presence.

Having the best sound and lighting with a flawless internet connection, perfect backdrop and slick framing doesn't make for a good presentation if your content is poorly laid out, overly fussy or badly structured. In this chapter, we'll look at how you should adapt your presentation content for online delivery - before we address the technicalities.

There are, of course, many different types of presentation - an hour long lecture is different to a sales pitch; a motivational staff presentation is different to a sombre review of a failed project - but poor presentations do tend to share the same characteristics you should look to avoid: too long, unstructured, fussy slides with too much text and delivered in an energy-sapping monotone. Just one of these missteps can undermine your entire presentation.

There are two key facets to discuss in relation to optimising online presentation content - the appearance and the structure of the material itself. Both need to be re-evaluated compared to a physical presentation but they share a common theme - simplicity. In an online setting, simplicity is always the preferred approach - so the slides need to be laid out in a clear, simple manner, and the concepts also need to be presented in a clear, simple manner. You need to (re)structure your material, mindful of shorter attention spans of online viewing audiences.

Know Your Audience

The content, of course, should be appropriate for your audience, but you need to consider carefully, for example, the suitability of online webinars for certain material, given the constraints your audience is likely to face. For very detailed information, it may be preferable to offer downloads participants can review at their own pace. For live online presentations, you face the twin challenges of scale and attention. Instead of watching a big screen in an auditorium, the majority of your audience may be in front of a 15" laptop or even a 10" tablet. They may be viewing in less than ideal circumstances - on small devices or with myriad distractions, compared to the typical giant screen and focus of an auditorium. Your virtual audience may even be eating, with half an eye on their email or even online shopping as you talk!

Bad presentations can be rescued somewhat in real life scenarios, where a good presenter's presence can mitigate unappealing slides but online it's likely that the slides will have to do more of the work. As you get more confident with online delivery and using the software though, don't be afraid to pause your screen sharing and take over the whole screen with your webcam view to address the audience more directly. This can make you dramatically more relatable than when you're a thumbnail image beside a slide.

Simple Design

Mark Twain is quoted as having said *'I didn't have time to write a short letter, so I wrote a long one instead'* and that holds true for presentations. A short, snappy presentation that still conveys essential information with compelling clarity is far harder to author than a long list of bullet points.

Much of the advice for good presentations stands also for good *online* presentations: make sure your slides are clear, relevant and not text-heavy. As I said, for online, simplicity is the ultimate sophistication; keep your slides simple, use minimum words, and prefer striking images where possible. And while variety is important, so too is some consistency or your presentation can come across as very disjointed. Every topic and presenter will have their own pace, but a good default is not to talk about a single slide for less than 1 minute or more than 3 minutes. It's ok to use a slide for less than a minute if it's an impact one or an image you're using to break things up, but too rapid cuts between visuals will leave your audience struggling to keep up.

Online, it's especially important to avoid jargon as you can't easily gauge if your buzzwords and acronyms are appropriate. Someone who may reluctantly signal to you in person that they are fuzzy on an acronym are even less likely to interrupt an online presentation.

For each and every point you want to make, you need to be ruthless. The aim is to ensure that only critical content makes it into the presentation - there needs to be no filler content. Without losing the core meaning, you need to cut back on the number of points - resist the temptation to add statistics or facts that reinforce points you've already made; duplication isn't a good use of limited space. I use two criteria to evaluate each slide's content:

1. would the presentation be worse off without this slide?
2. can I improve how this slide communicates its key point either visually or by reducing the text

Clear Layout

The start point for your online presentation design is to make the content as clear as possible on your audience's screens, bearing in mind how small the screens might be. Allow for larger borders on your slides - position the text more towards the centre of the slide than you typically would - it's possible that your slides may end up somewhat cut off on viewer's screens.

Use a plain background for your slides and focus each slide on only one point or idea. Don't crowd too many bullet points or text onto a slide. You ideally need the audience to look at a slide and get the point at a single glance - they shouldn't have to focus on "reading" it.

As always, resist the template tendency to push you towards bullet points as the only layout. Where you do use bullet points, bring each one up separately, so the audience isn't focused on reading ahead, but listening to what you are saying, with the slides playing a supporting role. Anywhere you use 'builds' (dynamic elements on a slide), resist transitions or fancy text effects flying around the screen. Instead of bulleted lists, consider a technique where you spread out your points over more slides, rather than less - reasonably frequent changes of the screen will help keep the audience engaged and reduce wandering attention.

Here's a before and after example of how to maximise impact and not follow the template that encourages filler bullets. The second slide will get your audience's attention and give you a basis to talk through the key finding rather than have your audience dutifully reading the bullets.

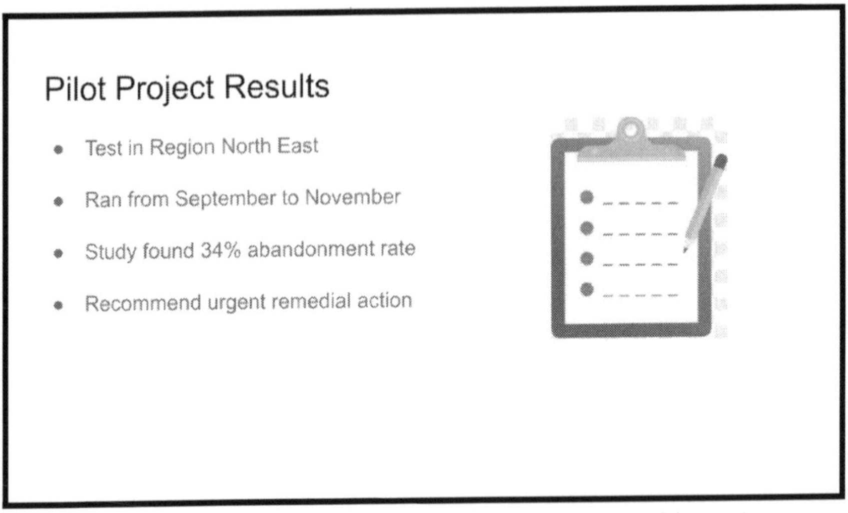

Pilot Project Results

- Test in Region North East

- Ran from September to November

- Study found 34% abandonment rate

- Recommend urgent remedial action

Figure 2: Before - A fairly standard templated layout

34%
Abandonment!!

Figure 3: After - a much more impactful slide with the key point

For text, larger fonts are definitely preferable - it's vital your audience don't end up squinting at their screens trying to read small text - increase your font size several points over what you might normally use.

If you're going to try any of the more advanced options discussed in chapter 9, these also need to factor into your layout choices - for example, if you're going to overlay anything on your slides, ensure it doesn't block any important content.

Images and Video

People are used to consuming highly visual information if they're in 'watching mode' (as opposed to reading mode) - so effective online presentations need to lean away from text/bullets and make much more use of images. Make use of full screen images with a short phrase making your main point and then talk to the bullet points you'd normally add. Don't think you've made your slide more visual by using your usual bullet points and adding a quick piece of clipart - photos will look much better - the cliche that a picture is worth a thousand words has a more modern version - an image is worth 5 bullet points!

For images, ensure that they are of good quality but not such high resolution as to make your presentation slow to load as it will look choppy on poor connections. When you're finished your slides, download a copy to check the file size. If it's big on your computer, it'll be slow over a virtual presentation too. Always make sure you have the rights to use an image, and credit the source in your notes.

While video can be an important part of many presentations, I'd recommend generally avoiding video clips as part of online presentations, as video played in an online platform such as Zoom doesn't always transmit smoothly to participants. However, if it's crucial to your story, make sure to provide a link to a copy of the video on YouTube or somewhere else so that anyone who had quality issues can review it later. Also, be sure to introduce the video with details of its duration so people know how long it will last. This provides valuable context for anyone who may be facing technical challenges - at least they know you'll be back presenting in x seconds or minutes, not that they are going to have to suffer through pixelated or buffering video for an unknown duration. If you do plan to use video, just make sure it's short and to the point.

People expect to have you present and add value, not introduce yourself, press play on a video and leave them to watch passively.

Similar to the point above regarding text borders, leave more padding (space) around images than usual too - for example don't put a graph axis label too close to the side of the slide - give everything more room to breathe than normal. Don't rely on complex graphics or charts that don't have very high contrast between data ranges. Brush up your Excel skills and whip up a quick chart instead of using a table unless there's a very good reason to favour tabular data. I can't stress enough the difference for an audience viewing your content on a 6" mobile or 15" laptop compared to a giant auditorium screen. Watch some webinars yourself on a phone or tablet so you can empathise.

Simple Structure

As well as changing the layout and appearance of your content, online presenting also requires you to reconsider the structure. Where a physical presentation may get away with starting slowly and building pace, that's a risky strategy for webinar formats.

Start Strongly

In an online world, first impressions count for a lot. Unlike a physical presentation where people are slow to abandon a session if that involves rather obviously standing up and walking out, online there are no such barriers - if people aren't hooked, they will quickly abandon the session or start to multitask. This makes the opening of your online presentation critical - you've less chance to win your audience back than if they were sitting in front of you with few (polite) alternatives.

It's always good to manage expectations and provide some context and structure with an agenda or overview of what you're going to cover in a talk but it's not the best way to start online. Just think how many presentations you've attended started the same dull way "Hi, My name is…..and here's the agenda for the next hour". Not exactly novel! Try instead to grab the audience's attention ahead of outlining the agenda - consider if one of these techniques works better than opening on a "Contents" slide:

- Start with a story - tell a brief anecdote (less than 1 minute) that's relevant and illustrates a key lesson from your presentation
- Open with a question to get the audience thinking rather than passively listening
- Use a famous quote that adds some gravitas to your position or indeed debunk a famous quote to create a sense of shock
- Display a shocking graph or statistic to establish how important the issue at hand is
- Show a prop that creates intrigue or adds tangibility to your concepts

It's a good idea to somewhat over-think how you're going to start - you should work extra hard on the first two or three sentences that you will utter. If you've delivered presentations in the past, you probably felt that after a minute or two you got into the flow of it and stopped thinking about the mechanics and focused on the content. Knowing your opening will help you bridge that gap, while ensuring your audience quickly feels your confidence and believes you know what you're talking about.

Similarly - though not to diminish the core of your content in the middle - you need to know exactly how you plan to close out. Make sure your last slide makes an impression. What's the *one* thing you want the audience to take away. Avoid ending on the feeble cliche of "any questions?". Be more direct and tell people *how* to ask questions - "Use the Raise Hand option and we'll unmute you to ask your question" or "Type your question in the chat box". Display a slide with a location for any downloads you promised or referenced and a contact details slide so people know how to email you, with queries or perhaps (hopefully) enquiries about having you come and speak at their next event!

Engagement and Interaction

As with any presentation, online presentations benefit from presenters who talk *to* the audience, not *at* them. I believe it's helpful to use phrases like "as you probably have seen" or "I can't see but I'm guessing there's at least a few of you who are nodding in agreement when I say". By addressing the audience, you can make them feel more involved. Pay careful attention to the advice in chapter 6 about looking at the camera. If you don't look at the camera, the audience will perceive you're not really talking to them and will quickly lose interest. It's easy as you stand alone in a room, seemingly talking to yourself, to forget how important it is still to include the audience.

A vital consideration for many online presentations is how you plan to handle audience interaction. I discuss this here under Content rather than in the next chapter on Delivery, as I regard the audience as playing a key role in your presentation. Online, they still can but you have to work at it - what was instantaneous and obvious like a show of hands has now become invisible or delayed. Though interactivity is in many ways harder online than in a physical presentation, as you can't look the audience in the eye or see a raised hand as easily, in other ways it levels the playing field - introverts who might not like to speak up in a crowded room are empowered from within their own homes.

Make sure you set the scene clearly about interaction and manage expectations. If you'd like attendees to ask questions, make sure the chat or relevant similar function of the platform is enabled. And manage expectations about whether you'll answer the questions in real time or at the end; the asynchronous nature of online platforms is actually a benefit over live situations - people can type their questions as they come up but you can leave answering them until the end so you don't break your flow.

The context, tone, scale, duration and purpose of your online session may determine the practicalities of interactivity but if you're extending anywhere beyond 30 minutes, it's probably nearly essential to maintain engagement. In fact, quite a lot of research suggests that 10 minutes is a good time to switch gears and involve the audience, even briefly, as that's the point where people's attention can really start to drift off.

Engaging the audience can be as straightforward as pausing, moving to a carefully designed slide, looking directly into the camera and addressing the audience with a rhetorical question or thought exercise. Breaking the flow from slide to slide and changing your cadence may be enough to snap the audience back from any drift.

As you get more confident with online tools, you can perhaps incorporate audience feedback - I don't recommend turning a serious presentation into a pop quiz, but it's worth considering adding some real-time polls to make the remote audience feel more involved. We'll discuss these tools in chapter 9.

Props

One technique I often use offline is to show props, to break the reliance on slides when presenting. I like to hold up something for the audience to see. If I'm talking about Artificial Intelligence, I like to hold up an example of a tiny handheld computer that can be deployed anywhere to do image recognition. If I'm talking about payments technologies, I might hold up my smart coffee cup that has an NFC chip in the base. As well as providing relief from the monotony of focusing on slides, it makes the concepts being discussed tangible or at least more visualisable.

If you choose to include props, they should always support your presentation content, adding value by making the idea more relatable. Online can make props a little tricky to use - check your webcam preview to ensure whatever you're holding is clearly visible. If you're interested in the idea and likely to depend on props in your presentations, check out the more advanced options in chapter 9 for sharing multiple cameras, which may help your audience get a better view of any props. Watch out, though, for virtual backgrounds (discussed in more detail later) - hold the prop directly in front of your body so it doesn't get blended into the virtual background and become invisible. If you're not able to use a live prop but feel it adds value to your presentation, maybe use a slide with a photo of you holding the item in question as that at least provides scale for the audience but also helps them connect with it if you're in the photo.

Highlights

If you're the kind of presenter that usually relies on a laser pointer built into your clicker, you'll find that particular aid taken from you in online presentations. There are alternatives - you can use the built-in highlighting tools in PowerPoint (Microsoft), Keynote (Apple) or Slides (Google) that let you draw on slides. This may be easier if you have a stylus-capable device, but watch out for vibrations if you're using your laptop webcam and trying to draw on the screen. If you're in an academic environment and heavily reliant on highlights, you might justify buying an external drawing tablet.

If drawing on a slide in real time isn't practical, I tend to animate a red circle to appear on note-worthy elements where I might previously have walked over to the screen and pointed on a stage. We'll talk in chapter 9 again about some of the advanced options more akin to this real-world experience.

Bring It Together

It would be a mistake to think that online presentations need to be dumbed down or somehow represent an inferior experience to physical events. While you absolutely need to adapt your content to the medium, it can challenge you to improve your clarity and communication in ways you wouldn't consider for a conventional presentation.

Remember that slides should remain a visual aid, not a script. Your slides are not your content - the story you tell, supported by your visual aids, is your content. If you take the time to create succinct, impactful, visually clear content, it's actually much more engaging for your audience and, selfishly, it's also much easier to present than text-heavy, bullet-laden slides. Include your audience as you design your materials - not as an after-thought - by ensuring there are logical points at which to interact. And when you're happy that your content conveys your message in the best possible way, it's time to move on to focus on how you deliver it to maximum effect.

Chapter 3: Delivery

From many of the online presentations I've watched in the last few months, it seems as though some people take 'online' as an excuse for 'lower standards'. While I've total empathy with people who are struggling through incredibly challenging times, I still believe it's important to make the effort to be as professional as possible in the circumstances, particularly if you're presenting to large audiences. As we all get more used to working in these strange times, presenters should take a moment to assess what incremental actions you can take to improve your presentation - your audience will appreciate your professionalism.

Whether you're a presenting novice taking advantage of the new ways of presenting or an experienced performer, it's useful to have a quick reminder of the basics, the important things that are constant whether you're presenting in person or online. Sometimes, it's the most obvious things that are the easiest to forget under the pressure of presenting in unfamiliar ways. But if you mess these up, it's very unlikely that even expensive technology will be able to redeem your professional image.

Style and Substance

Great content still needs great delivery. If you think that your work is done by following the content advice in the previous chapter, I'm afraid that isn't enough to make the most of online presentations. The whole dynamic of presenting online can feel very alien and the experience can sometimes be underwhelming for the audience if you don't adapt your delivery style, as well as your content, to the new medium.

Online presenting relies a lot on how you present yourself on camera. Although you should lead with your high quality content, the way you appear to your audience and how you deliver your content will influence their engagement and retention.

Camera or No Camera?

I've come across people who think it's ok to present online without switching on their webcam. While it might be an exaggeration to compare it to turning up to give a physical presentation wearing a face mask, not turning on your webcam is going to alienate your audience. A good quality video feed makes you more engaging as an online presenter, just as a live audience in the same room as you expects to see your face.

You can decide to switch your webcam off after the initial introduction has been done so that the audience can then focus on your content, but I'd recommend you stay on screen as much as you can. People invariably assess the presenter, as well as what you're presenting, to determine the credibility of the message.

If you're one of those very camera shy individuals or circumstances simply dictate that video isn't possible, at least have a simple slide with your photo and credentials on it which you can show when you open and close, as well as during Q&A. The more you can make yourself visible -- and not just a disembodied voice -- the more engaged your audience will be.

Nervous presenters may seize on the chance to present without a camera feed and just share their screen. While that's tempting and understandable, and perhaps acceptable for an audience who know you (e.g. colleagues or students), it's really not an option for a professional presentation. Remember that the camera represents the audience; it provides a focal point for you to present to and is your only means to connect visually with the audience by "looking them in the eye". If you're uncomfortable with it, practice until you get used to it.

If you feel that the camera isn't doing you justice, I'll explore the ways to improve how you look on camera in chapter 7.

Vocal Delivery

When the audience can't see you, your voice is left to carry a much larger load. Despite the great efforts I've advised you to put into creating great visual aids, ultimately your voice will be the decisive tool in bringing the presentation to life for your audience. We'll devote the entirety of chapter 6 to the technologies to best capture your voice but here I want to discuss how you deliver your content - what are you creating for the microphone to capture?

It's not just what you say, it's how you say it

"Words mean more than what is set down on paper. It takes the human voice to infuse them with deeper meaning"

–Maya Angelou

"The tongue can paint what the eyes can't see."

–Chinese Proverb

Your voice is a powerful presentation tool, capable of subtle, yet decisive, influence over how your words are received. Presenting effectively isn't just talking to your slides - you need to harness the flexibility of human speech to add impact to your words.

Voice modulation refers to how you control or adjust your voice. It's when you choose to go louder or softer, faster or slower, add emotion or drama. Alongside these controls, a formal presentation requires the speaker to put more effort into vocal characteristics such as articulation, pronunciation, inflection and projection than is common in daily speech. Happily, these come more easily with practice and become second nature - I once had a colleague who said it was like I had a switch for "presentation mode" and started talking differently anytime I was put in front of PowerPoint!

Enunciation

In general, I don't recommend or favour an overly formal presenting style - I think speaker authenticity is crucial and so, unlike some presenting guides/coaches, I'm not opposed to the use of colloquialisms or regionalisms or using contractions that would be considered "poor" enunciation. I know I'm certainly guilty of the odd "I'm not gonna" instead of "I'm not going to" and while I don't aim for poor articulation, I think it's less disconcerting for most audiences than sounding forced or false.

I do think it's useful for presenters to spend some time learning basic linguistics and being aware of how they speak on a more technical level, but I believe it's important to be selective about what you decide to change in your speaking style - the ultimate aim is to convey your message to the audience. As long as you are understood by your audience, then I'm not concerned by lack of perfect diction.

Later in this chapter, I'll recommend recording your practice presentations. When you review your session carefully, you may learn vocal tendencies you never knew you had - do you elide syllables in words subconsciously? (Elide is the linguistic term for the slurring or omission of a final unstressed vowel that precedes either another vowel or a weak consonant sound - vegetable, temperature or comfortable are common examples). Do you speak more monotonously than you thought?

Inflection and Emphasis

A monotone delivery is more off-putting than normal in a webinar that's already struggling for your viewers' attention. More than ever, it's crucial that you don't simply read out a PowerPoint presentation. Online, you need to inject more energy, sound like you mean it, sound like you care and want to inform your audience.

Inflection - the change in the pitch or tone of your voice - is key to making your delivery more interesting and effective. While adding vocal variation will make your talk more agreeable sounding, inflection plays an important role in conveying meaning and emphasis too. If you're not convinced about its importance, try this short exercise. Read the sentence below aloud and each time, place your emphasis on the *italicised* word to hear how it changes the meaning.

"*I* did not say she found the money" - Creates doubt - What did you say or Who did say it?
"I did not *say* she found the money" - Did you perhaps convey it some other way?
"I did not say *she* found the money" - If not her, then who found the money?
"I did not say she *found* the money" - Was she given it, or perhaps she stole it?
"I did not say she found the *money*" - Maybe she found something else?

Pace

Experienced presenters are usually good at pacing their presentations - their slide deck has a nice flow with just the right quantity of substance. And they've practiced carefully to finish on time. Pace and your content are inextricably linked. You need to choose your content based on the duration of your slot, which will be impacted by your pace. If you speak too quickly, you'll finish early and probably leave confused listeners in your wake; if you speak too slowly you'll over run, not complete your presentation and have lost audience members to boredom.

Pacing correctly is difficult for virtual presentations. Without the visible audience as a gauge, it's hard to know if they're struggling to keep up or impatiently waiting for more. The upside of virtual presentations, though, is that it's easier for you to have a prominent clock positioned where you can see it.

Figure 4: I keep a clock prominently positioned when presenting - and a second clock if I'm presenting to another time zone to remind me to adapt any time of day references

Online you should speak a little faster than you might normally, without speaking so fast as to leave the audience no time to absorb what you're saying. But a slight increase in tempo, with well-placed pauses, provides greater energy. Practice your presentation until you can reliably deliver it within the intended time slot.

Pauses

Traditionally, pauses are an important tool for presenting: skilled presenters use strategic silence and pauses to add to the effectiveness of a presentation. Online you need to consider their use more carefully - just as radio presenters avoid "dead air" due to the lack of a visual connection with audiences, online you may want to use pauses more sparingly and use facial or hand gestures to ensure the audience knows it's intentional.

Pauses are useful to both the presenter and the audience - they give you the opportunity to separate your thoughts and give the audience a chance to absorb what you are saying. Longer pauses (1-2 seconds) can be very powerful - they force the audience to think about what you just said and the change in pace is also a way of regaining the audiences' attention.

Without a signal from an audience, there's a temptation as an online presenter to keep talking for fear of an awkward silence. However, your audience will appreciate pauses or it can end up sounding to participants like an endless stream. Take a breath between sentences, or use strategic pauses to help emphasis or to reinforce a point. Although I emphasized the importance of shorter and simpler content in the previous chapter, reflect again on the fact that, from a delivery perspective, spoken sentences also need to be simpler and shorter than what can be comprehended by reading. If you haven't before, check out the book *"Eats, Shoots and Leaves"* for a reminder of the importance of punctuation and remember that inflection and pauses and other vocal modulations are your punctuation when presenting.

Volume

Another benefit of presenting from home is that you have more time to check the sound levels. Although professional venues usually have good sound systems, most experienced presenters will tell you horror stories of the times they've been expected to address a crowd of hundreds with no amplification or when the sound system has distorted their voice.

Most good presenters don't shout, but project their voice appropriately. But they will sometimes (sparingly) vary their volume for effect. Lowering your voice is a staple trick to emphasize importance - just make sure you don't lower it too much - check your sound levels and ensure your audio setup can cope with your intended range of volume.

Preparation

We'll talk later in this chapter about the importance of practice in the days ahead of presenting, but here I want to emphasize the role of preparation just ahead of your presentation delivery. I've seen countless nervous speakers pacing up and down whispering their content to themselves before going on stage and then struggling to get the words out. The most impressive professional speakers - that you think can deliver without a second thought - are the ones you'll find exercising their voice ahead of going on stage.

Preparing yourself to deliver your best vocal performance requires a mix of exercises across your body, breath and voice. As many people get nervous before a presentation, it's especially important to relax and reduce tension. Take a few moments ahead of your start time to shake any tension out of your arms, neck, shoulders. Roll your shoulders and roll your neck a few times. Take several deep breaths.

Just as a jogger stretches to limber up before a run, anyone about to embark on an important presentation should warm up their voice; actors often spend half an hour doing vocal warm-ups. Taking some time to warm up increases blood flow to the larynx and the other body parts that will deliver your speech - your lungs, lips and tongue. Especially if you're going to talk for 30 minutes or more, this preparation will reduce the chance of developing hoarseness and it also enables you to reach a wider range of pitch, which is important for the inflection and vocal modulations discussed above.

It may feel silly, but nowadays you can do these vocal exercises in the comfort of your own home before you begin - surely an advantage over trying to find somewhere to prepare at a conference venue. Start with some humming, and then recite some tongue twisters. Blow some raspberries (more technically known as a lip trill), roll your tongue and rub your jaw joints (saying their proper name - temporomandibular joints - is a bit of an exercise in itself). Just five minutes of care to limber up ahead of presenting will make a noticeable difference. Try it!

With your voice warmed up and ready to go, make sure you're well hydrated - the caffeine you might have chosen to raise your energy level can also dehydrate your throat. If you're seated, make sure to avoid slouching as good posture will aid your breathing. These simple tips will both protect your voice and ensure it's in top shape to present.

Physical Delivery

With your voice ready to bring your presentation to life, it's time to make sure you're ready to go on camera. Just because presentations are happening online doesn't mean you shouldn't put time and effort into your appearance and posture.

Wardrobe

Although casual dress has become standard for many people working from home, my rule of thumb for presenting is to wear what you would have worn if delivering the presentation in person. Despite the changed setting, that's most likely to be appropriate and to set the tone with the audience. Wearing your "work" clothes will also act as a subconscious reminder to you that you're on the stage, albeit virtually - that's not a sense you're likely to have wearing a t-shirt and shorts.

The new dimension to consider, apart from how formal you want your wardrobe to be, is how suitable it is for being on camera. Although even the worst modern cameras are less prone to moire patterns on clothing, it's still a good idea to avoid distracting patterns, stripes or checked designs. It's also preferable to skip shiny fabrics such as silk or satin as they can appear very reflective on camera and make lighting harder. Simple solid colours (though not black or white) are ideal to keep the focus on your content more than your clothes and not over-exercise the exposure controls on the camera.

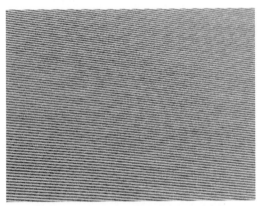

Figure 5: Some patterns don't work well on video creating a moire effect - I don't wear this shirt when presenting!

It's also a good idea to remove jangling jewellery for the duration of the presentation - bracelets can easily rustle or bang against the desk, while necklaces may be audible, especially if you are wearing a lavalier mic, as we'll discuss in chapter 6, where we'll also look at mic-mounting techniques if your clothes don't offer easy mic positioning.

Stance

Most home offices start with a chair, desk and a laptop or monitor as the focal point. And while that may be suitable for email, Excel and even team meetings on Zoom, it's not ideal for presenting. Depending on the purpose of the presentation, and the duration, I strongly recommend you consider standing instead of sitting. This is one of the most basic techniques that people overlook when seeking to improve their presentation.

If you think about it, it's very rare in physical presentations for the presenter to sit. Yet we default to sitting for online - anchored to our computers. Standing has several physical benefits - it makes it easier to breathe and helps you project your voice more clearly. It makes it less likely you'll be too close to the camera (more on that problem in chapter 7). It also allows for natural gestures and looks less rigid. That increased energy comes across to your audience, even if it feels odd to stand in front of your desk at home, or at your kitchen counter!

Standing may increase the technical challenges we'll talk about later in terms of camera and microphone positioning but the payback is huge - you'll differentiate yourself and come across far more energetic and engaging and far less monotonous than other, seated presenters. Physiologically, standing creates a different energy compared to sitting. It conveys more confidence.

When I present on stage, I love to pace around but that's not an option for online presentations - if you do stand, you need to stay still and move as little side to side as possible. One trick I use is to put a guide on the floor to remind me to stand on it. If you haven't already tried it, I strongly urge you to try standing for your next presentation - assuming you can do so in line with the advice in the upcoming sound and video chapters - I think you'll be surprised how much of an impact it has. Your audience will pick up on your energy - if you expect them to be engaged and energised, you have to be too. Standing helps address that new challenge of conveying that energy without physical presence.

Figure 6: Always use a slide remote – models range from £20 to £100

If you're standing, it's unlikely you'll be able to reach your computer easily to advance your slides, so you'll need a presentation remote. Even if you are sitting, though, you should still use a remote slide clicker. Especially if you're using your integrated laptop microphone, just pressing a key to advance your slide can sound noisy to your audience as the keyboard noise is amplified. Likewise, the vibration of your laptop can come across as a disproportionate shake on your integrated webcam. And a slide remote also gives you the ability to change the slide while gesturing. Also, if you've a touchscreen laptop, don't touch the screen to advance slides either as it will vibrate the integrated webcam!

Your Energy

When discussing vocal preparations above, I mentioned the importance of relaxing your whole body. As well as focusing on your voice and ensuring you don't sound monotonous, you can engage your audience by exuding energy. It helps if you have enthusiasm for your topic, but stress, nerves or your mood can obscure or dampen your energy as perceived by the audience.

Use whatever you find works to give you an energy boost - sugar, caffeine, a banana, or a Red Bull, so that there's no fear of lethargy creeping into your performance. I always try to get some fresh air before a presentation - even if it's just opening a window - but preferably by getting a quick walk around the block before starting. Use a full range of physical gestures when speaking – even if they can't be seen clearly on camera, they come through in your voice.

Your mood is also evident from your voice - people will be able to tell if you're tired or not in a good mood - and that transfers as a subtle lack of persuasiveness as you present. If you need a mood boost ahead of the presentation, try watching some funny YouTube clips to distract yourself, meditate or call a friend for a chat - whatever perks you up.

Practice!

Presenting can seem deceptively simple but professionals take great care to practice and refine their techniques so as to appear effortless. If there's one take away from this book, it's the importance of practice and preparation, while adapting to circumstances as best you can. Don't take presenting for granted and just sit down in front of your laptop as if you were about to type an email!

Practice will make you a better presenter and will also give you the chance to identify, prioritise and mitigate challenges posed by your environment, software and equipment, as you look to make the best possible pandemic presentations. As I said earlier, presenting is a learned skill - practice is guaranteed to build your confidence - practice works! Even if it feels unnatural, you need to practice. Even if you're an experienced presenter, practice more. Audiences can tell the difference between someone who has practiced and someone who hasn't.

I recommend a few different phases of practice, each focused on different areas of your delivery. It's useful both to practice by yourself and to practice with others. I always go through my presentation in a dry run in advance of delivering it, even when I think it's finished and ready to go; it invariably throws up some slides that don't work as well as I thought they would.

Practice Recordings

Having practised, the key phase is now to record yourself, ideally on the platform you'll be using to deliver your presentation - typically Zoom, Meet or Teams. If you don't have access to the exact platform at the time of practice, then use whatever tool you have handy.

While you may initially cringe somewhat as you watch yourself, it's a great way to spot things from a viewer perspective that you'll miss when simply running through your slides. Look for slides that are too busy or unclear, look for distracting mannerisms that you didn't realise you had and pay particular attention to how you look and sound as the recording is the closest approximation of what your final audience will experience.

The more you practice, the more comfortable you'll become with the different tools of pandemic presenting - how best to use the camera and microphone, which presenting aids in the software you prefer and identifying any areas you find difficult. I also recommend asking colleagues, friends or family to watch you present and to comment constructively, but critically, to help you identify areas for improvement. Go through the experience of sharing your screen, until you're completely familiar with the platform you're using. Don't assume that because your presentation on Zoom last week went ok that everything will be ok on Microsoft Teams next week. Practice! While it may seem tedious, it's always worth a few minutes to confirm that something works as expected in advance rather than be faced with the credibility-undermining experience of publicly figuring out how the technology works as hundreds of people wait for you to start and your slot ebbs away.

If at all possible, practice in the same room you'll present in, with the same lighting, the same Wi-Fi, the same camera and microphone setup you'll have on the day of the presentation. As you review the video of yourself presenting, look at it critically but constructively. Ask yourself the following types of questions:

The Absolute Basics:
- Does it look right - am I clearly visible?
- Does it sound clear - can people hear me?
- Are my slides easy to see, with everything visible, even on small screens?
- Is the content duration too long/too short?

Delivery Style:
- Have I used enough inflection/tone changes to avoid monotony?
- Am I using enough/too many hand gestures?
- Is the pacing ok - is it upbeat but not frantic?
- Have I used interactivity to break things up?

Beware of complications as you add more technology - you may inadvertently end up confused, connected to the wrong microphone or camera. Test again after every change you make to your setup.

Live Recording

It's really useful to be able to look back at recordings of your actual sessions to see how you delivered them compared to how you rehearsed/expected to deliver. And you can use that content online for social media promotion or your portfolio. Be cognisant of peoples' sensitivities around recording. While you may want to record the session, unless you have participant agreement, you might want to end the recording ahead of any Q&A session so nobody withholds a question for fear they'll be recorded.

Watch and Learn

While I strongly recommend you spend time recording and watching your own presentations for areas to improve, it's also extremely helpful to watch other presentations critically - see what works, what doesn't work for other presenters. Is there anything you can learn from their style, their slides or their delivery? Attend some webinars - make sure you know what it's like to join an event and get the attendee perspective. Identify what you dislike as an attendee so you can make sure not to do that in your own presentations. If you see a presentation you particularly like, reach out to the speaker on LinkedIn (or via email if they've published an address) if you want to understand what tool they used. I'm always ready to share tips if a fellow speaker contacts me after seeing me presenting.

Rehearsals

Rehearsals are important! If you're speaking at a well-organised online event, you'll likely receive an invitation to attend a technical rehearsal. I've seen experienced speakers objecting to being asked to do technical checks ahead of presentations, but I always agree and, in fact, *ask* for such preparations. Although I've addressed thousands of people via Zoom and other platforms during the pandemic, and have invested more than the average person in technology to optimise the quality for people who watch and listen to me, I still know that each time can be different.

Some platforms favoured by organisers of large events may require you to login in a slightly different way, while others have a green room area where you can wait "backstage". So always make sure you know what the flow is - talk to the host beforehand, instead of getting a surprise on the day of the event.

Ready to Go

The tips in this chapter all come without a budget - being a good presenter is a learnable skill and has a lot to do with preparation and practice rather than investing in expensive equipment. In the Covid-19-impacted world, it can also have a lot to do with improvisation and making the most of what's available. Even if you want the support of additional technology, many of the items for online presenting are in high demand with uncertain supply.

Once you're ready to present, it's time to consider where you'll present from - how are you going to find and set up the best place in your home to present?

Chapter 4: Environment

Presentations used to take place only in spaces designed especially for them. Now, even the most important presentation may be originating in a far-from-ideal makeshift 'stage' in the corner of a busy household. Presenters can no longer expect to turn up for an event and be greeted by a rostrum or podium in an acoustically designed auditorium with perfectly tuned amplification and giant displays to captivate their audience. But that's not to suggest giving up on finding the best possible spot in the circumstances. It's worth doing a little reconnaissance tour of your home, looking afresh for characteristics you would never have worried about - acoustics, lighting and locks on the inside of the door!

There's now an entire sub-genre on YouTube of inappropriate interruptions of TV interviews as people working from home are surprised by the arrival of their children or pets in the midst of a serious discussion. And while everyone understands the realities, it's not the professional image you're likely to want to portray on a regular basis as a presenter. Depending on your individual setup, it may not be possible to prevent such interruptions entirely, but with a little planning and communication in the household, it's usually feasible to secure a safe location for long enough to present.

Location

Deciding where in your home works best will likely be a compromise. Remember that the place where you normally sit and work may not be equally effective as a presentation 'stage'. And while moving your laptop and setting up elsewhere may seem like a lot of effort to give a 30 minute presentation, if it improves your stance, the sound, your lighting or reduces interruptions, the effort will be rewarded with a much more professional presentation appearance.

2020 has seen a dramatic increase in sales of PCs, monitors, headsets, webcams and desks as well as home gym equipment and home office equipment, as people hurriedly try to create a better work environment. But as you plan any acquisitions to better equip your home for work, it's important to consider if there are more fundamental environmental changes you can make, if presenting is going to be a significant part of your activity.

If you're lucky enough to have a room you can commandeer for presentations, that will likely give you more scope to adapt your surroundings than if you can only manage a temporary loan of a space. Consider all your options - check the basement, attic or garden shed if you're lucky enough to have those kinds of spaces.

Room Choice

Let's assume for a moment that you have the luxury of a choice of spaces at home that might work - ideally, what characteristics would you look for? The physical environment has a big influence on how you'll come across online. Huge amounts of design effort goes into the creation and optimization of professional presenting spaces to ensure they're suited to the task, with good sound, lighting, furnishing and presenter amenities.

- If you've a choice between room sizes, err on the size of smaller. It's easier to dampen the echoes in a small room than remove the hollow reverb you get in larger rooms.
- Favour carpet or soft flooring over hardwood floors. Hardwood floors both create echoes and can also be noisy if you move on them. If your whole house has hard floors, see if there's a rug anywhere you can use for the duration of the presentation.
- If you have to choose between a room that offers good lighting and a space that's quiet, opt for the quiet space as it's easier to improve your lighting than reduce unwanted noise.

Pause and listen carefully for the noise from any appliances - alongside heating and ventilation, one of the noisiest appliances in most houses is the refrigerator, so avoid sitting near one, if possible. If you have the option, you can also turn off your air conditioning or heating fan for an hour. We'll return more to acoustics in the chapter on sound, but you can prepare for that by looking for rooms with soft coverings - for example, curtains absorb more sound than blinds.

Do Not Disturb

Once you've decided on your environment, consider how best to secure it. Does the door have a lock to prevent unexpected intrusions at inopportune moments? If there's no lock, a low-tech solution of a hanging Do Not Disturb sign, similar to what you might use in a hotel, may be enough to signal to your housemates that you need privacy.

There are higher-tech solutions that might both prove more intimidating to intending trespassers and come with the added benefit of remote control - you can turn on a warning light from your desk at the last minute, whereas you might forget to hang the sign on the door before you're live on air. How much effort to expend depends on how permanent your setup is, and how likely interruptions are. Among the options are USB-powered status lights designed for office cubicles or something like a Philips Hue Play lamp that can change colour to warn off would-be invaders.

Figure 7: (L) A simple busy indicator light (USB cable to computer) and (R) a wall mounted, Wi-Fi controlled light

Furniture

The sudden advent of working from home has led to a surge in demand for desks, as well as a stream of photos on social media of improvised home office configurations. Most of the attention has been on creating the most suitable work environment for conventional seated work, for productivity and for meetings. Even professional presenters spend most of their time on these sorts of tasks, handling email and creating content. But, as we'll discuss, presenting online is rarely optimally served by configurations for other kinds of work.

While some advisors will tell you to start by getting a new webcam and microphone (and as you'll see in the later chapters, they're probably correct), there is a strong argument that you can make a significant gain in presenting performance simply by elevating your laptop or finding a desk or countertop at a more suitable height. After elevating the camera, I find one of the next most beneficial environmental benefits when presenting is a printer stand that I've repurposed to sit beside me, just out of camera shot, that contains my clicker, glass of water, props, backup microphone and other accessories. This simple piece of furniture makes things run smoothly and leaves me to focus on delivery.

Ventilation and Air Quality

If you are hidden away in a small room that was never intended to be occupied in this manner, it may also be worth checking the air and environmental conditions. Again, compared to a professional venue that has expensive HVAC environmental controls, your spare room or attic may not have ideal conditions, especially for prolonged use.

At a basic level, try to ensure the room is well ventilated and at a comfortable temperature. You'll probably want to close any windows while presenting to avoid external noise, but make sure it's well ventilated before and after your presentation. This may seem like one of the overkill situations I warned I'd mention, but if you're focused on your presentation and the technology, you may not notice if the atmosphere deteriorates. Poor air quality may impact your breathing and energy levels without your noticing. Slightly too much carbon dioxide in a poorly ventilated room can make you drowsy, while if humidity levels are too low, you may become parched. If this is your semi-permanent home office where you spend upwards of 8 hours a day, it's potentially worth checking the environment - the venues we were used to frequenting before stay at home orders take their air quality seriously.

Indoor air quality is often significantly worse than outdoor air, yet we often don't pay much attention to ensuring the air quality in our homes is optimal. If your budget allows, consider a simple air quality sensor and then a humidifier or air purifier if indicated by the sensor. You won't be able to run these devices during your presentation (too noisy) but you can make sure the air won't make you drowsy when you present.

Figure 8: (L) An Awair air quality sensor and (R) a Meross smart humidifier

Environment Summary

When presenting from home, you're more on your own than usual. In a business or conference setting, you usually have a more permanent setup tailored to presentations, or at least people who will provide the basics (such as power leads, batteries or just bottles of water). When presenting from home, you need to supply these essentials yourself.

I also see it as an opportunity - you have much more flexibility to make the space work for you. Post-it notes are your friend - often a staple of office stationery supplies, they may not be readily to hand at home, but I'd recommend ordering a few packs. This is the time to take advantage of the things you can't do on a physical stage - plaster the space in front of you with Post-it notes reminding you of key things to say or do.

If possible, ahead of a presentation at a venue, I would always check out the room. How does the stage feel? Is there something odd about the podium? Are there any poorly positioned spotlights that are going to beam directly into my eyes? Is there room to pace?

At home, the good thing is you have more control over the setup and more time to consider everything. You can make sure the podium is wide enough and you can make it the height you prefer.

Finally, if you're in a smart home, turn off your Alexa, Siri or Google Assistant devices - just so they won't start talking if you happen to say their name or something like it during the presentation! Speaking of technology, let's move on to look at the technology that you may have or may need to shine online....

Chapter 5: Computer & Connectivity

Suddenly, a lot is being asked of home computers and especially laptops. Devices built to constraints around cost, portability, slimness, battery life or weight are being asked to undertake static assignments that value few if any of the characteristics that make for a desirable laptop. If you were to design a computer that didn't have to move around, could be continuously plugged in, was easy to attach a high quality microphone or camera to, you'd design....a desktop machine! Or you'd design a very different laptop - prioritising a top quality web camera, for example, instead of compromising on quality to fit one that doesn't add even an extra millimetre to the depth of the ultra-portable laptop lid.

As a decreasing number of people have a desktop machine at home, I'll assume in most cases here that people have a laptop with a built-in camera and microphone. If you've a desktop, then you may already have had to source external devices such as a camera and microphone, or you may have an All-in-One (AIO) desktop design, in which case the same advice for integrated cameras and microphones for laptops applies.

Computer

We'll talk more about the key AV elements (microphone and camera) in the coming two chapters, but it's important also to review the basic configuration and capabilities of your computer as they relate to online conferencing. Not surprisingly, focusing exclusively on the camera and microphone capabilities required for a high-quality Zoom, Teams or Meet presentation but ignoring the computer they're attached to could seriously undermine your efforts to maximise technical performance.

A computer specified for typical email or spreadsheet workloads may not be up to the challenge of all-day conferencing. While it may not be practical to buy a new laptop now, there are things you can do to improve the performance of your current hardware and features to look out for next time around, if home-based presenting is going to continue to be a requirement for you.

Working with what you have

The good news is that most recent computers, with just a few tweaks, have enough capability to run quality online meetings. Some slightly older or budget models may struggle a little or be unsuitable for some more advanced features but there are a number of universal tips to get the most out of your hardware.

CPU and RAM

The main chip (Central Processing Unit - CPU) at the heart of your computer is an important determinant of your online conferencing performance. Together with the memory space it has to work with (Random Access Memory-RAM), your processor is responsible for processing your sound and video, displaying your slides and managing the connection to your conferencing platform.

How do you tell if your computer's CPU is struggling? Well, if it's slow and choppy (unresponsive or jerky), if the fan is on all the time, that might be a sign that heavy duty video conferencing is at the outer end of the computer's abilities. If the processor is overwhelmed, your video and audio may appear choppy on your audiences' screens and your PC may be slow to respond when you want to advance to the next slide.

The first thing to do to help your CPU, when presenting, is to relieve it of other tasks - shut down any applications you aren't using. Note that many laptops in particular are configured to prioritise battery life over performance but this isn't a concern if you're at home with your laptop plugged in. Check your power settings to make sure that power-saving measures are disabled and performance is prioritised.

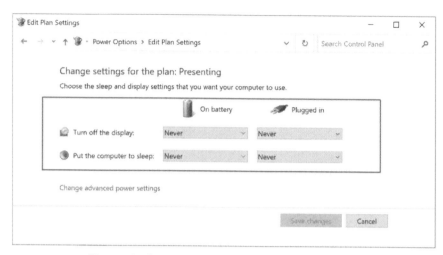

Figure 9: System Power Settings on Windows

Settings

While you're looking at these settings, make sure that your laptop isn't set to go to sleep or dim the screen after a few minutes of inactivity - if someone in the audience asks a question and you stop moving through your presentation to answer them, you definitely don't want your laptop to go to sleep! Another setting to watch out for is updates - Windows, in particular, has a habit of insisting on taking control of your machine for updates that take ages to install. So, make sure you have the appropriate schedules chosen for updates and the PC doesn't start an hour-long installation 10 minutes before you're due on air!

What CPU do you need for online presenting?

Each piece of software you use will have requirements for resources from your computer hardware. Remember that you'll be running not only your slides software (PowerPoint, Keynote, Google Slides, etc) but also your Conferencing client software (Google Meet, Zoom, Microsoft Teams, etc) and asking your computer to process your sound and video, so it can add up to quite a computational load.

Zoom, for example, has a detailed list of minimum specifications on their web site but remember these are minimum and you should ideally aim above them - additional CPU power and RAM will make it easier to run PowerPoint and any additional software you might need or want. If you're using virtual backgrounds, note that these require lots more CPU and RAM than no background. If you're moving into the Professional/Advanced level presenting or have ambitions beyond presenting into podcasting or vlogging, you should consider the most powerful CPU you can afford with generous amounts of RAM.

Zoom recommends Dual-core 2Ghz or higher (Intel i3/i5/i7 or AMD equivalent) but goes on to note: "Dual and single-core laptops have a reduced frame rate when screen sharing (around 5 frames per second). For optimum screen-sharing performance on laptops, we recommend a quad-core processor or higher"[4]

If your computer is struggling to keep up, laptops unfortunately don't have upgradeable CPUs but you may be able to add RAM. Desktops are much more likely to have upgradeable CPU/RAM. If you are buying a new device and if you can stretch your budget, remember to spec it a little more generously than you might have previously, as it will make your presentations that bit smoother as well as future-proofing your system for a bit longer.

Two Monitors

It's not strictly a computer, but a key part of your setup and one of the simplest ways to make things easier when presenting online is to invest in a second screen - attach an external monitor to your laptop or add a second monitor if you are using a desktop. This is because, even though most presenters address their audience directly when in an auditorium, in an online presentation, you're drawn to look at your slides. As we'll discuss in chapter 8, the second monitor lets you see your presentation on one screen while looking at your online platform or audience on the other. A second monitor doesn't have to be particularly high specification but you can pick up a 24" monitor for about £100. If you're short on space, there are some very neat and light portable second screens designed for laptops, starting at a little over £200.

---

[4]https://support.zoom.us/hc/en-us/articles/201362023-System-requirements-for-Windows-macOS-and-Linux

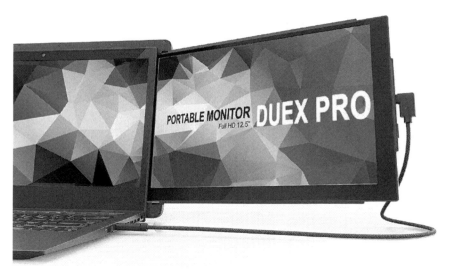

Figure 10: Attach a second monitor to your laptop if you need a compact solution for about £250

Connectivity

Arguably more important than any other aspect of your hardware setup is your broadband connection. Without a solid internet connection, many of the other measures in this book will be rendered useless - there's no point having great lighting, perfect sound and an expensive camera if your internet connection isn't up to speed.

Home broadband has been more important in 2020 than ever before. Previously vital to keep the family entertained and to keep the online shopping deliveries flowing, fast and reliable home internet connectivity has in many ways made the pandemic lockdowns somewhat bearable, certainly more so than they would have been even ten years ago. It's been possible for most people to keep things going, working and schooling from home, ordering essentials, maintaining social contacts and keep being entertained.

Your Broadband Plan

In areas that have cable or fibre broadband available, even the basic packages will provide sufficient speed and capacity for most households. For example, in my area, the basic cable package offers 250megabit download speed and 25megabits upload, with unlimited data. Note that upload speeds are important in a conferencing scenario as you're sending your video and slides up, not just receiving Netflix!

While I have an unlimited data plan, check for any allowance or other constraints on your package as Zoom, for example, will use the following amounts of data[5]:

Video Quality	Data Download	Data Upload	Total Data Transfer
High	450 MB/hr	360 MB/hr	810 MB/hr
720p	675 MB/hr	675 MB/hr	1.35 GB/hr
1080p	1.2 GB/hr	1.2 GB/hr	2.4 GB/hr

Although Wi-Fi has become the dominant means of commencing to the internet in homes, cabled connections are still preferable for high performance devices. That's why games consoles, for example, favour ethernet cables over Wi-Fi connections. It's increasingly uncommon to even have ethernet connections on laptops, but, if you have one available and can run a cable to your

---

[5] https://www.reviews.org/internet-service/how-much-data-does-zoom-use/

router, it's the better option. If you don't have a port on your laptop, you can easily get a USB to Ethernet adaptor for about £15.

Wi-Fi Setup

Assuming your basic connectivity is good enough and you don't have a cable option, the biggest performance influence may be your Wi-Fi setup. Although your ISP will supply a Wi-Fi Access point, it may not be optimal. However, there is a large range of dedicated Wi-Fi devices to ensure better coverage within your whole house.

Range

As many people retreat to the attic or even the garden to find space to work from home, previously adequate Wi-Fi configurations are coming under strain. If possible, move closer to the location of your Wi-Fi router. You'll notice a significant decline in speeds the further you are from your router, or the more obstructions (walls) between you and the device. As mentioned, if you can revert to a good old-fashioned wired ethernet connection from your computer to your router, then go with that. (It may require an ethernet to USB adapter, as fewer laptops these days include ethernet ports). If you are exceeding the number of your laptop's USB ports as you add more accessories and therefore need to use a USB hub, make sure it's a powered one.

If you can't move closer to your Wi-Fi, consider a Wi-Fi extender solution. There are whole house "mesh" Wi-Fi solutions from brands such as Google Nest, Amazon's Eero and TP Link Deco. You could also try Powerline adapters which use your electrical wiring to speed signals between rooms.

Device Priority Setting

Even if you have a good broadband connection and strong Wi-Fi signal around the house, it's still worth trying to ensure your presenting device isn't competing for bandwidth resources when it needs it the most. Most of the Wi-Fi setups mentioned above come with the ability to prioritise one device temporarily - so your laptop won't lose out to the kid's XBOX. If you can't implement a technology-based priority, you may want to negotiate with anyone else in the house who wants to stream games or 4K Netflix during your presentation.

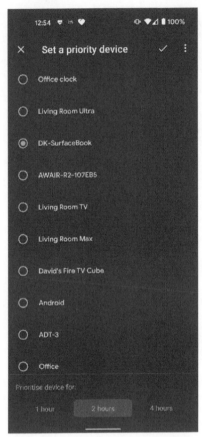

Figure 11: My Nest Wi-Fi allows me select my laptop for priority Wi-Fi access

Hardware Summary

I'm sure we'll see a range of work-from-home/conferencing-optimized devices on sale in the coming months as hardware makers look to service this new market segment. Meantime, all but the oldest computers can likely handle running Keynote and Zoom or PowerPoint and Teams. Take a few moments to optimise the settings to give them the best performance, while ensuring your connection to the Internet is also as strong as possible. If you can, do consider adding a second screen - you'll thank me for presenting purposes, but I'm sure you'll appreciate the extra screen space for other tasks too.

Chapter 6: Sound and Microphones

After you've made the most of your existing equipment and environment but - perhaps within a limited budget - are looking to improve the perception of your online presentations, I'd recommend starting with improving the sound quality and specifically upgrading your microphone hardware.

Although initially you might instinctively think that improving video quality is a better starting place for an online presentation, in fact most online sessions have more focus on your slides and your voice than your camera feed, so the quality of your camera may not be quite as important as the quality of your sound. If your video isn't great but at least if your sound is good, participants can still listen to you. As the Zoom website states: "in cases of compromised bandwidth, Zoom will prioritize your audio over your video to make sure you're heard."[6]

For most people who may be watching your presentation, nothing is more off-putting than poor audio quality. Regardless of whether it's distracting background noise, or just bad audio quality, poor sound undermines your credibility as a presenter, hinders engagement and means you're unlikely to be asked to present again.

Good Sound Matters

As you listen to presentations, podcasts or watch TV shows, you're probably not even aware of good sound - it's something we take for granted. You likely don't appreciate the effort that's gone into ensuring crystal clear sound. But while good sound is something you don't generally notice, bad sound is something you very quickly do and it can be fatal for an online presenter. If the audience loses video, it may be possible to continue with just sound. But lose sound, and you've lost the audience for sure.

If you've ever seen inside a radio studio or a recording studio, the lengths they go to there in order to capture the best quality sound are quite extreme. The entire environment is usually covered in sound absorbing materials, with every care taken to exclude

[6] https://blog.zoom.us/working-from-home-tips-to-meet-like-a-pro/

extraneous noise sources. Expensive microphones are carefully mounted and positioned for minimum vibrations and carefully measured distance to the source of the sound. There's a reason that venues and broadcast studios do what they do - the trick here is to find the biggest bang-for-your-buck lessons, techniques and technologies that can transfer from the studio to the home environment.

Most of us regularly use tiny microphones without any thought as to how they work. We expect our smartphones to capture and transmit our voice with high fidelity. Although not typically a primary marketing point, a lot of effort has gone into equipping phones with high quality microphones - in most cases, multiple microphones are used to ensure the best quality sound. (The iPhone 11 for example has 3 - one at the top, one at the bottom and another on the rear). And that's in a situation that's somewhat kind to microphones - we almost always hold them very close to our mouths, which is key to reducing extraneous noise.

More recently, many people have come to expect their smart speakers to hear them even when addressed across a room. Unbeknown to most users, these devices use sophisticated far field microphones with beamforming technology to react, whatever the distance from the owner. However, the microphones available to most people for online presenting are far less sophisticated than what you might find in an Amazon Echo or Google Home device. But the shift to home working has suddenly made us really notice for the first time the quality of the microphones in our laptops and, in most cases, these are far from optimal.

In this section, we'll discuss the variety of sound-related options you might consider, based on your budget and needs:

- Focus on the audience experience
- Microphone Fundamentals
- Microphone Options
- Microphone Accessories

What the Audience Hears

Before we explore a little the technicalities of microphones, it's crucial to remember microphones aren't about your experience as a presenter; they are the first crucial link in capturing and transmitting your content to your audience. The microphone may pick up things you don't hear as you present. The microphone may accentuate things you don't notice or elements that make your presentation harder for people to listen to and therefore less effective. It's easy to assume that you sound fine to your audience, because you sound fine to yourself. Alas, that's not always the case.

It's not always obvious to you, but small changes can make you a lot more listenable to on the listener's end. You might not hear your hissed 'S' or plosive 'P' but, as we'll see in the accessories section, sticking a £10 pop filter in front of your microphone might be worth it if it improves the sound for a few listeners. Again, it's not about what you hear - it's about the audience.

People are frequently surprised when they hear their recorded voice for the first time - "do I really sound like that?" is the common initial reaction. But what's even more surprising is how you sound over platforms such as Zoom or Google Meet. That irritating background hum you don't notice is muffling your voice for the audience. The clicking noise as you tap your foot, that's transmitted through your desk to the super sensitive new microphone you're so proud of as the solution to make you sound professional, is annoying and distracting your audience.

In comparison to a room where you can judge directly if attendees can hear you (and it's a singular location so you know everyone has the same experience, except maybe those in the back at a large venue), it's a very different story when you are talking to maybe thousands of people in thousands of different locations, each with a different setup and connection. Some may be forced to turn up the volume on their end or listen on poor quality speakers so the better the original quality, the less distortion at the receiving end. The sound has a long way to travel and must navigate a lot of potential transitions and technologies along the journey to its final listener; that makes it really important to maximise the quality at its origin. Having left your mouth, your words will be encoded, encrypted, transmitted, amplified and (hopefully) finally turned back into audible, intelligible vibrations for the listener's speakers or headphones.

Acoustics

Your basement, attic or box room, commandeered as a makeshift office, is highly unlikely to have been designed with good acoustics in mind. And while the sound may seem ok to you, the echoes typical of domestic rooms may be distracting or unpleasant for your viewers/listeners. While you may upgrade your microphones in search of better-quality voice, a more sensitive microphone is also likely to accentuate echoes you never noticed. The good news is that sound reflections can be absorbed, which is why recording studios feature soft carpeting, foam walls and draped curtains. I'm not recommending everyone rush out to buy studio grade sound panels to cover their walls, but even a few old blankets draped around the room can help eliminate the "empty" sound of your room.

Referring back to the room choice section earlier, the size of the room also has a lot to do with your acoustics. If the room is too small, it can cause more noticeable echo, which will probably make people ask if you're presenting from the bathroom. Conversely, if you're set up in a room that's too large, reverb can make it sound like you're recording in a cave. If possible, try to base yourself in a medium-sized room with soft sofas and curtains that will absorb rather than reflect sounds. The better the mic, the less forgiving it will be of the room - e.g. it will pick up sound reflections from the room. So, the downside of buying a better mic is that if you go too far, you'll introduce new problems and potentially require some additional investment to mitigate these.

Background Noises & Distractions

Sometimes, people don't think about background or ambient noise when they're presenting online, but microphones (good and bad) can pick up all manner of undesirable extraneous noise. I've talked in earlier sections about trying to ensure you're not interrupted, but even if someone doesn't burst into the room unexpectedly as you're in full PowerPoint flow, you need to take a moment to ensure that the washing machine or dishwasher in the next room isn't reaching the peak noise part of its cycle at the worst moment. The clothes or the dishes can wait until you're finished.

Even if you've secured your environment from yelling kids, howling pets or screeching machines, there are myriad audio dangers closer to the microphone. If you're sitting as you present, make sure your chair or its wheels aren't squeaky - WD40 is your friend in tracking down rogue squeaks! Listen out too for vibrations on your desk - particularly if you're nervous/excited about your presentation as you may jiggle your feet or knock against the desk with your hands. The simplest way around this is to avoid these bad habits but if not, look at the 'Mounting and Shielding' section later in this chapter for helpful accessories. And remember to mute your microphone if you feel the need to cough - but don't be the person who needs to be told to unmute!

Don't despair if you can't find somewhere that's the ultimate in quietness. Working from home has its realities —whether it's a barking dog, a blaring car alarm, a passing helicopter, or someone mowing their lawn right outside your window, you can't expect total isolation. But factor in your ambient noise challenges when choosing your microphone and accessories - the right choices may help to offset problems.

Microphone Fundamentals

Although microphone options can get quite complicated - and I don't want to try to turn you into a sound engineer instead of letting you focus on presenting - it is useful to understand a few fundamental concepts and terms if you want to make good microphone choices.

In this section, we'll talk about microphone types, polar patterns and connectors. More technical evaluation criteria for microphones such as frequency response, impedance ratings, diaphragm size and sound pressure levels (SPL) are not usually relevant for domestic/office use and you can likely ignore them as you research your preferred microphone purchase. You may see these terms and specifications if you're researching high-end microphones, but they are typically only of concern in more challenging conditions such as live music venues or when micing complex instrument setups.

Microphone Types

Although they might look simple enough, microphones are actually quite complex devices. Different underlying technologies can be housed in similar-appearing devices. I won't go into the mechanics of how each type works here, but it's useful to know some of the terminology and rule out options that wouldn't suit you. Even if you don't intend to change from whatever mic you have, understanding the basics of characteristics will help you get the most of it, and to know why it behaves the way it does. The important thing for presentations is that you'll want a mic focused on good voice quality - many expensive mics are actually targeted at musicians and are better at recording instruments than voices, so don't buy on price alone!

Microphones are categorised based on (1) the underlying transducer technology they use to convert the air pressure variations of a sound wave to an electrical signal and (2) the direction(s) from which they are designed to pick up those sounds, referred to as the polar pattern.

Types: Condenser & Dynamic

The two most common types are *condenser* and *dynamic* microphones. If your research takes you deeper into microphone technicalities, there are also *ribbon* microphones but they are fragile, costly and rare outside studios.

- Condenser mics are the most common mic type you'll encounter. They are more sensitive (not always a good thing!) than dynamic mics with extended frequency response ranges, which makes them suitable for recording vocals and instruments such as pianos.

- Dynamic mics tend to be a bit more robust than condensers (and cheaper), which makes them popular for live events, as does the fact they can handle higher volumes, making them suitable for loud instruments.

If you have a musician in the house who already has a mic you are planning to borrow, their mic may be good quality, but it may not be ideally suited to Zoom use, as different types of mics are better suited to music/instruments than voice. That said, if you have a good dynamic mic available, there's no need to rush out and replace it, but if you're buying especially for presenting from home, condenser is probably the better choice. Refer also to the section on Connections below, as you may need an adapter to attach the mic to your computer if it is intended more for instrumental recording.

Polar Patterns

Polar pattern is the term used to describe the direction(s) from which a microphone best picks up sound. This is useful to know for several reasons:

- Which is the optimum direction to speak into the microphone - i.e. does it have front/back
- Is the microphone susceptible to picking up background noise?
- Is the microphone suitable for two people to use simultaneously, e.g. in an interview situation

Understanding the polar pattern should help you position and address the microphone in the most ideal way. Knowing the characteristics of your microphone should help you maximise the pickup of your intended source, and hopefully reduce extraneous sources. It may also influence your choice of accessories which we'll discuss later.

There are 4 main types of polar patterns commonly available:

- Cardioid
- Bi-Directional
- Omni Directional
- Unidirectional/Shotgun

The diagram below shows the direction of sound each will pick up, with the mic at the centre of the image.

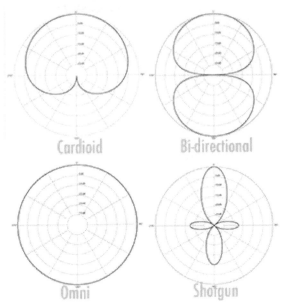

Figure 12: Polar Patterns

Cardioid

The 'cardioid' polar pattern is the most common, so called due to the shape resembling a heart. It focuses mainly on a single sound source direction to the front of the microphone, with minimal pick-up from the sides and rear.

Bidirectional (figure-of-eight)

Bidirectional (also known as figure of 8) microphones, pick up a near equal level of sound from the front and the rear, with little sound from the sides. They're used primarily in interview situations, so if you're looking at doing interviews for a podcast and then looking for a presentation mic, a switchable device between cardioid and bidirectional is likely ideal.

Omnidirectional

Omnidirectional microphones pick up sound equally from all directions in a near perfect sphere. Typically, omnidirectional microphones include most lavalier (clip on) and headset varieties, as they allow the wearer to move their head without altering the overall sound of the recording. Omnidirectional mics are less liable to pronounced proximity effect (see next section).

Unidirectional/Shotgun

With a tighter pattern than cardioid, the shotgun microphone has a narrow, very focused pick-up area - sounds from the sides will be largely ignored. Shotgun mics are typically used when trying to pick up a specific sound at a distance, and are often seen mounted on top of a camera but are not favoured for indoor use as it's usually preferable to place a mic closer to people when they are speaking rather than relying on long-range pickup. Although they are perceived as very directional, they do typically still pick up some sound from behind.

Some microphones have switchable patterns, which means you can pick the one most appropriate for a given circumstance.

Figure 13: Switchable polar patterns on the popular Blue Yeti USB microphone (c £120)

The difference between a cardioid and omnidirectional pattern, for example, becomes crucial in meeting rooms - hence it's not usually as simple as swapping microphones from one context to another. A mic that performs well picking up voices around a table is not ideal for use to capture a single front-on speaker in a noisy environment, so if you were thinking of borrowing a conference room mic from the office for home use, that mightn't be a good idea technically (or something that would make you popular with your colleagues or office asset manager).

Placement and Addressing

Choosing and acquiring the most suitable microphone for your requirements, budget and situation isn't the end of the story. With an understanding of the polar pattern, you should now be able to get a head start on how best to position the mic in ideal circumstances. This may require an accessory of some sort, though as we'll see, many popular mics come with stands, and virtually all mics can be adapted for use in a wide variety of mounts that help you maximise their pick up characteristics.

Ideally, a microphone should be about 6 to 12 inches away from your mouth and angled up towards your mouth. If the microphone is too close to you, it may cause your voice to sound muddy and difficult to understand. If the microphone is too far away, you run the risk of sounding hollow or distant, which can also make you difficult to understand.

Simpler microphones won't typically have any controls on them (maybe not even an on/off switch) but where they do have controls, it's a good idea to make sure you know what every dial and button does. Most important, make sure you're speaking in the right direction! With most microphones, you want to aim at the side with the brand label. Some models, especially dynamic mics, need to be addressed from the top. This may sound very basic but remember the microphone polar pattern determines where it will pick up the sound - other than omni-directional mics, all sides are not equal. If you have an existing mic and aren't sure what its polar pattern is, you should always start by testing it with the logo facing towards you as side-address (as opposed to top-address) designs tend to display a logo.

Proximity Effect

Most microphones exhibit a change in sound quality depending on how close they are to the sound source. The 'proximity effect' is an audio phenomenon where the low-frequency response increases the closer the mic is to the sound source. If you have ever spoken into any mic you've noticed how much louder and deeper your voice gets as you move the mic closer to your mouth. Rap and hip-hop artists use the proximity effect when recording to get a rich deep vocal tone - I'll leave it up to you to determine how suitable that is for your presentation and audience! Cardioid mics exhibit the proximity effect more than other mics.

Microphone Settings

After finding the perfect microphone placement, it's time to check the settings on your computer. Make sure you've selected your USB microphone as the input source in your conference software. All too often, people have their lovely new USB microphone plugged in without realising the software is still using the built-in computer microphone.

Next, it's time to tweak your microphone settings. Many mid-price and high-end microphones offer a variety of switchable settings, including pickup pattern and microphone gain, which is the boost level the microphone applies to the input signal it detects. For example, the £120 Blue Yeti microphone has a gain dial, while the £50 Blue Snowball doesn't. If your microphone doesn't have a gain setting, you can still adjust the sound level in the software; if your microphone has a gain dial, you'll need to set gain on the microphone *and* in the software.

Start by selecting the most appropriate pickup pattern for your environment. Then, adjust the microphone gain to make sure your voice isn't too loud or too quiet when it reaches your computer.

If your microphone has a gain control, start speaking at a normal volume, and then slowly turn up the gain knob until you start to see a signal on the level meters on your microphone or in your conference software settings. Continue to increase the gain until the signal on the meter starts to reach the yellow or red lights and then turn the gain back down a little. The gain should be set so that the meters reach the top of the green section during the loudest moments of your conversation, but never reach the red lights. We'll discuss some of the other audio settings in chapter 8.

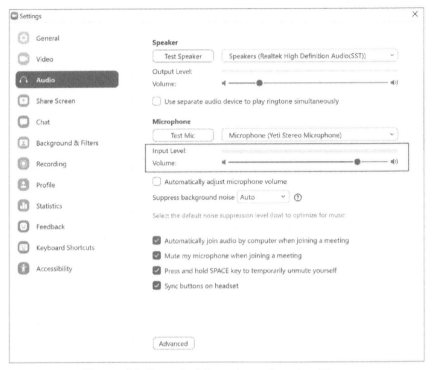

Figure 14: Zoom's Microphone Input settings

Microphone Connections

A final technical consideration, before we move on to talk about the shapes and sizes of available microphones, is what type of connector the microphone has, and if it's easy to connect it to your laptop (in most cases) or external camera (if you're using a DSLR camera as described towards the end of the next chapter).

As microphone connectors were historically designed primarily for supplying sound to recording devices, they weren't envisaged for widespread use connected to laptops and smartphones and so, for example, the standard professional microphone connector type (XLR) is far too large to fit in a modern laptop, let alone a smartphone.

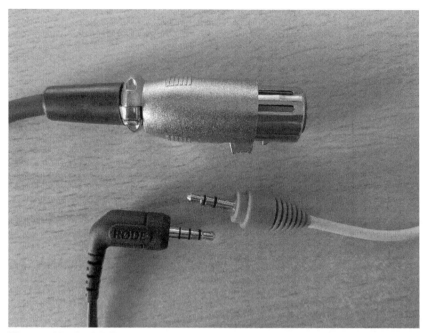

Figure 15: An XLR connector (top); Similar looking TRS (middle) and TRRS (bottoms) 3.5mm connectors

As shown above, there are 3 sizes of connectors you may encounter when evaluating audio equipment:

- 3.5mm (TRS or TRRS)
- XLR
- USB

XLR

High quality microphones tend to come with XLR connectors commonly used in studios. This robust connector can only transfer analog signals which are of no use to a computer. You therefore need an adaptor or interface to convert the signal into a digital one and to connect to a PC using a standard (for computers) USB cable. You can get an XLR-to-USB converter (see example below) if you have an existing mic, but, when buying new, if it's only ever going to be connected to a computer for online presentations and conferences, then it's simpler just to get a mic with a USB connector. If however, you're intending to set up a multi-microphone solution for podcasting interviews or recording music, you may want XLR microphones for easier connection to a mixing desk.

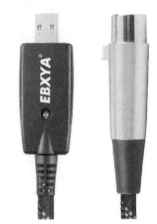

Figure 16: XLR to USB Cable

3.5mm (TRS/TRRS)

Confusingly, there are two types of similar looking small 3.5mm jack connector types you may encounter on microphones. These are much smaller than XLR but also aren't generally suited for connecting to laptops, which increasingly lack dedicated microphone ports in favour of more flexible USB connections.

- TRS is the type of connector usually found on a DSLR camera for microphone input and is the standard type of connector you'll typically see on lavalier (clip-on) and shotgun mics designed for use with DSLRs.

- TRRS look very similar to its TRS counterpart but includes an additional connection. This is because smartphones require an additional connection to enable both the left and right channels for the headphones along with the microphone, so TRRS can be used on headsets with microphones for making phone calls, such as headsets supplied with most smartphones.

When it comes to using mics with a 3.5mm jack, such as lavalier microphones, you need to pay close attention to what kind of output your microphone has and what kind of input your recording device has – specifically, whether they are TRS or TRRS. Some manufacturers colour code their plugs to help differentiate them, but adaptors are available between the two formats.

USB

Although USB is near ubiquitous for connecting accessories and peripherals to computers, microphones, as we've said, are analog devices and were largely designed in the era before USB so USB isn't native to microphones. Connecting via USB to a laptop is actually a slight technical challenge for a microphone and you can't just connect a mic that wasn't intended for that purpose. As mentioned, there are adaptors (with an analog to digital converter built in) to convert mics to USB if you have a high quality XLR mic available. Designed for-USB mics are characterised by their ability to do analog to digital (A/D) conversion within the mic so they can connect directly to a computer. The A/D converter is usually hidden inside the mic, but in smaller mics, such as a lavalier, you'll notice the USB plug is larger than normal to house the additional circuitry. The quality of this A/D conversion is vital to ensure the sound you hear is as close as possible to the quality recorded by the mic and is strongly influenced by the price you pay. The conversion quality depends on the audio bits and sample rate - most USB microphones offer 24-bit and 96kHz sampling rate with cheaper devices rated at 16-bit/48kHz, which will offer lower sound quality. A premium device such as the Blue Yeti Pro (£250) adds ultra-high 192kHz resolution.

Microphone Options

Now that we've covered the technicalities of microphones and the factors that affect their performance and suitability, the next part of the microphone journey is to look at the shapes and sizes they come in.

Adding a better microphone is, thankfully, easy and starts at a quite affordable level, though rapidly increases in price if you want more sophistication. As we'll see in the next sections though, there are also a number of accessories that can enhance the performance of even an average microphone, which may be a better choice than simply buying the most expensive microphone you can afford.

Integrated

First things first - when you've done everything from a content and setup point of view to improve your presentation quality, you likely need to improve your microphone hardware. The microphone built into your laptop was never intended for prolonged use or for making presentations. Most laptops include only cheap microphones, frequently hidden from view given their historical lack of importance. Their somewhat perfunctory inclusion means they usually aren't ideally positioned to pick up voices clearly, while they are doomed to pick up the fan noise, as well as amplify any noise such as rustling papers on the desk/surface you're using.

However, you may not be in a position to acquire new microphone hardware, so let's first look at how to make the most of your integrated mic if that's all you have to work with. While I strongly advocate not using your integrated microphone, all is not lost if that's not possible for you. Indeed, there are some premium laptops with fairly respectable integrated mics and your laptop may have some settings you can use to tune your mic's performance.

A useful step is to locate the whereabouts of the mic in your laptop - this may require a Google search for your laptop model. Strange as it may seem, it can be quite difficult to locate the mic on a modern laptop. As previously unimportant components, they rarely feature prominently, and are often hidden, which can lead to their being inadvertently obscured. When you do locate it, make sure it's clear of obstructions and be extra careful bumping the desk or tapping in close proximity to it. Tips like elevating the laptop which may primarily be aimed to help the camera, can also give the mic a boost - a laptop stand may help simply by moving the mic away from vibrations on the desk.

Figure 17: A simple laptop stand can help isolate your laptop from the desk, bring your microphone closer and bring your camera closer to eye level, while improving ventilation which can reduce fan noise

Many webcams offer integrated mics and while these are generally not as good as a dedicated mic unit, they are certainly preferable in most cases to the ones built into your laptop. If nothing else, they will be further away from the laptop itself, better isolating them from noises and positioning them closer to the speaker's mouth. We'll talk more about webcams in the next chapter.

As a premium laptop, MacBooks tend to have slightly better mics than other laptops. But as you can see below, a quick comparison of even a MacBook Pro mic module beside a £50 entry level external mic shows how much more room is available in the external unit for components to capture your sound accurately.

Figure 18: A MacBook mic module (L) compared to an external mic (c. £50)

Headsets

While integrated mics in laptops may struggle to deliver good performance, there are already devices in many households that include better quality or better positioned microphones that can improve your online efforts: headphones or earphones.

The first thing many people will turn to are the earphones that came with their phone, or, in the case of (formerly) frequent travellers, their fairly high-quality noise-cancelling headphones that also include microphones. Popular wireless buds such as Apple Airpods or Google Pixel buds can be paired with laptops that have Bluetooth. Of course, you need to ensure they are charged as they are unlikely to have enough power to last an entire day, but they can do several hours of presenting/video calls on a charge. An affordable wired USB headset with a mic for £15 will likely beat your laptop integrated mic, while the Logitech Zone is a popular wireless option but runs around £200.

One solution I've found works well and is more comfortable/less obtrusive than earbuds is a device like the Bluetooth Bose

Soundwear - literally a wearable speaker that sits on your shoulders but positions a microphone near your mouth, while leaving you unencumbered by a cable and, if you match your outfit to the (changeable) colour cover on the Soundwear, isn't as visible to viewers as things sticking out of your ear.

Figure 19: Headsets for all budgets : (Top-L) Bose Headphones (£200), (Top-R) Bose Soundwear (£200), (Bottom-L) Wired USB headset (£20), Logitech Wireless Headset (£200) (Bottom-R)

I must admit that personally, as a viewer, I don't like the look of visible headsets or headphones on presenters. As a presenter, I feel it leaves you cut off from the environment - you may not hear external noises that your viewers will hear. But for attendees, I also think it looks unnatural - they may wonder what you're listening to though, in fairness, it may help you focus or hear better in a nosy environment. But headphones are still absolutely preferable to poor quality sound, so if that's your best mic option, don't hesitate. Headphones do bring the added benefit that there's no risk of feedback from your speakers as you present.

Desktop Microphones

Most mics aimed at home use are intended to be mounted on a desktop stand of some sort - many popular models will come with a basic stand. Though intended for desktop use, most can also be mounted in other ways as we'll see in the next section. As mentioned, due to the popularity of podcasting and game streaming, there is a larger range of quality audio hardware than ever before and, as you research your best option, you'll frequently see desktop microphones targeted at Podcasters and Streamers as you research your best option.

Popular desktop models offer significantly better sound than laptop integrated solutions (without any of the complications of wearable mics we'll discuss in the next section) and can be easily positioned out of sight of your camera but within range for clear pickup of your voice in most seated and standing configurations. Many mics are also attractively designed, so you may not want them out of shot!

Starting at around £30 and going up to £150 and (way) beyond, it's thankfully hard to go wrong with many of the top brands offering good sound and instant USB connectivity. Here are some example popular models from budget to premium prices:

	Amazon Basics Desktop Mini	Marantz Umpire	Blue Yeti	Blue Yeti Pro
Price (Typical)	£25	£50	£120	£200
Type	Condenser	Condenser	Condenser	Condenser
Polar Pattern	Unidirection	Unidirection	4 patterns	4 patterns
Bit/Sample Rate	16/48kHz	16/32-48kHz	16/48kHz	24/192kHz
Connection	USB	USB	USB	USB or XLR
Stand	Included	Integrated with Shock Mount and Pop Filter	Desk mount included	Desk mount included

Space can be a consideration when choosing a mic for your home desk – as you can see in the photo below, some models are quite large. Smaller models such as the Samson Go (£50) mic can clip onto your laptop if a desktop model is too big when space is at a premium on your home presentation 'podium'.

Figure 20: A Blue Snowball (Left), Amazon Basics Mini Desktop (Centre) and Blue Yeti (Right) with a 13.5" laptop for scale

As mentioned, I'm a fan of standing when presenting, which makes a desktop mic slightly less practical. It's still far better than an integrated one and if well positioned, can still work. I've found it perfectly workable to position a desktop mic near me but still out of shot, which does offset some of the cons of wireless (battery life/signal interference) or wired clip-on mics (cable), while retaining the freedom to stand. But you do need to be disciplined not to move away from the pickup pattern of the mic, which is another reason to implement my tip of placing a marker on the floor.

Lavalier

Lavalier or 'lapel' microphones are one of the best ways of getting a mic close to the speaker and a favourite of professional audio technicians when recording dialogue. These clip-on mics offer proximity to the sound source (i.e. your mouth) which eliminates a lot of the difficulty in achieving good signal from a desktop mic.

Figure 21: A Lavalier clip-on mic

Connection wise, lavaliers typically have 3.5mm TRRS jack connectors but there are TRS, USB and Lighting (iPhone) models available for connection to laptops, smartphones and iPhones. Watch out if you're tight on USB socket space on your laptop, though, as the USB models can have larger than normal plugs (for the A/D converter mentioned earlier) meaning it may not fit in your laptop alongside another USB device.

Mounting

Lavalier mics are typically very small, intended for discrete mounting near the presenter's mouth - as a general rule, placing the mic capsule over your sternum will give you a nice balance between close proximity and natural sound reproduction. Moving your lavalier microphone closer or further from the mouth will have a noticeable impact on sound quality. Professionals tend to mount lavs upside down inside the mic clip to reduce the noise from plosives and fricatives (which we'll discuss more a bit later). Watch out for potential rustle if you allow the mic to rest against the clothing or skin - the clip or mount should keep it slightly elevated.

Lavs are usually supplied with a simple mic clip that attaches to a physical edge of clothing, such as a jacket lapel or button-up shirt. Another type of lavalier clip is the 'vampire' clip. This design has two pins that can be used on a piece of clothing such as a t-shirt with no suitable grip area for a standard clip. These particular clips will be visible to the camera, so you may want to practise good cable management and ensure both the mic and cable look neat and tidy. Industry veterans use techniques such as the 'broadcast loop' where they create a little slack in the cable at the clip to help to diffuse the vibrations.

Figure 22: (L) A Broadcast Loop with standard clip and (R) Lavalier "Vampire" Clip

Concealing the Lavalier

Definitely in the territory of overkill for most online presentations, but for perfectionists and perhaps for those regularly hosting a video podcast, hiding your mic can give a clean professional look that's ultimately less distracting. A black lavalier mic can be quite noticeable on white clothing (though white lavs are available), and as viewers, we're less accustomed to seeing visible mics as most professionals try to hide them.

If you need to conceal your lav microphone beneath clothing, it is common practice to use a variety of tape techniques to stick the mics out of sight. A more complex mount is something like the RØDE invisiLav which is a transparent rubber mount for lapel mics, designed to be stuck to the presenter's clothes or skin under clothing to conceal the mic capsule while absorbing vibrations caused by movement. But be careful not to hide your mic too well and end up muffling the sound! A visible mic with clear sound is always preferable to a carefully hidden one that's not as clear.

Headset

Lavalier style mics can also be mounted on a headset for positioning beside your mouth. The cable can then be run down the presenter's back to a computer or a wireless transmitter. For example, mic maker Rode offers a stainless-steel headset mount that weighs just 5g for their lavalier range if you prefer this option over a clip-mount.

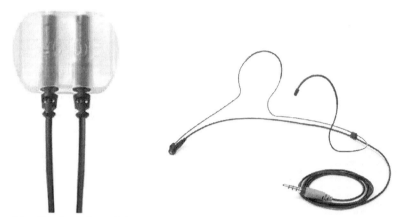

Figure 23: (L) Invisilav Stickable Mount (£15) and (R) Headset Mount (£25) for Lavaliers

Wireless Lavalier

Because I prefer to stand when presenting, my personal mic choice is a wireless lavalier clip-on unit. This saves me having to stand where I can have a well-positioned desktop or boom-mounted mic and negates any of the more cumbersome cable management solutions. I use the SmartMike+, which is a compact Bluetooth unit, clipped to my shirt and it lasts for about 5 hours on a full charge. Wireless does introduce a battery issue so it's important to include charging the mic battery on your checklist and to always have a backup wired mic, just in case.

Figure 24: Bluetooth Wireless Clip on Mic (£110)

While the unit I use is a single small unit containing the mic and transmitter, many solutions have the clip-on capsule unit separate from and connected to a transmitter unit that needs to be clipped on the presenter's body. As described above, there's an industry tendency to try to hide cabling and that also applies to the transmitter but, while that makes sense on stage in a theatre, it's really not necessary on a business presentation.

Camera Mics

Before we go on, in the next chapter, to talk about cameras in more detail, let's briefly talk about cameras from a sound perspective as many external cameras also include microphones.

If you already have access to a high quality DSLR with a TRS input and a "shoe mount" (an accessory socket on top of the camera), it could influence your mic choice as you might find it most convenient to use a shotgun mic on top of the camera. While cameras often have a small on-board microphone, this seldom provides good quality audio, picking up echo and many other extraneous sounds and for presentation use offers little improvement over the integrated microphone in a laptop, especially as the camera is likely to be further away from you.

Figure 25: A mini shotgun mic mounted on a DSLR camera

Mounting and Shielding

I believe the vast majority of online presenters will see a dramatic - and sufficient - improvement in their audio output quality by investing in a budget or medium level microphone. Out of the box, these microphones will offer much higher quality than any integrated laptop microphone.

For presenters with specific challenges or constraints, there is however a range of accessories that may help with particular environmental issues or more flexible placement preferences. These are generally unlikely to be necessary for pragmatic or even polished presenters but may offer some incremental improvements in special circumstances.

Depending on what and where you plan to record, you might need to consider adding one of the accessories discussed below - a different mount, a pop filter, or perhaps even a shock mount to your mic. You can easily spend more than £100 on those three items alone. For some users, a mic that ships with its own stand and wind screen or pop filter (such as the £50 Marantz Umpire USB) will be the more reasonable choice. Before you buy a new mic, do check what accessories come with your choice. Also, look out for bundles too as these have become popular in recent times, to offer aspiring podcasters simple one-click solutions.

Desk Stand

Good mics are bigger and heavier than you might imagine. While many come with a stand, others leave it up to you to choose one that suits your surroundings. It's important to get a solid stand so your mic won't fall over, especially if you add any extras such as a pop filter or shield. It may feel logical to put the mic between you and the laptop, but you might be better to place it slightly to one side of the laptop as you can get reflection of your voice bouncing off the screen, particularly with an omnidirectional mic.

Although I'm all in favour of repurposing other household items to improve presenting, note that you can't simply repurpose a camera tripod due to the different size of microphone mounting threads (¼" vs ⅜"), but you can order an adapter.

Boom Arm

Those with the luxury of a large, dedicated desk may opt for a desk mounted boom arm that they can swing out of the way and not take up space in front of the screen. Favoured for podcasters or YouTube presenters, If you're lucky enough to have the space, this is probably the ultimate setup - there's a good reason that it's what you find in radio studios, as it enables careful repositioning of the mic as needed, can accommodate sitting and standing, and isolates the mic from knocks, while being moved out of the way when necessary.

Amazingly, you can get boom arms starting at about £10, though a more robust one might run closer to £100. You might try a cheap one if it's temporary or even just for a couple of events, before investing in a more durable solution. Boom arms are usually supplied with a twist screw to attach non-destructively to a desk or table so you can set them up and tear them down quickly.

Figure 26: A microphone boom arm

Sound Shield

In most home situations it's neither practical nor desirable to install the kind of sound proofing used to improve the acoustics of a dedicated broadcast studio. However, there are domestic-appropriate devices that can be used to mitigate issues in less than ideal sound stages.

A simple foam shield reduces unwanted ambient noise and sound wave reflection without requiring structural changes to your home or decor! There is a variety of collapsible shields you can add to a desktop mic setup - you can even erect a shield around your laptop. Your shield can be a standalone unit, or it can be installed on your mic stand if the stand can hold the weight of the isolation shield without tipping over. Shields typically come with standard microphone mount points and are more necessary for more sensitive microphones, or if you're struggling with background noise or an echoey room.

Figure 27: A sound shield can protect your microphone from unwanted noise. Prices start around £30

Pop Filter

Even if you're not familiar with the phonetics terms plosives, sibilants and fricatives, everyone has heard public address announcements marred by loud popping and banging noises, even though we never hear these noises when people speak normally.

There are certain letter sounds (known as aspirated plosives) such as B and P that mean we expel small blasts of air, which can be picked up by microphones positioned very close to our mouths. Try holding your hand an inch in front of your mouth and say a word that begins with B or P - you'll feel a puff of air that isn't there if you say a word that begins with a letter such as D.

While it's usually necessary to have your microphone fairly close to your mouth for the clearest sound, it increases the intensity of the plosive sounds for the microphone and the hissing of sibilant 's' and 't' sounds. This is further exacerbated by the 'proximity effect', where microphones are notably more sensitive to low-frequency sounds from very close sources.

In most professional recording contexts, you'll see circular nylon-mesh screens that clip to the mic stand and sit a couple of inches in front of the mic - a pop filter. These cheap devices (from less than £10) can reduce or eliminate distracting noises, particularly if you're prone to over-pronouncing your plosives. If you get a pop filter (which you can attach in front of any type of desk or stand-based microphone), try the trick with your hand again - put it behind the pop filter and notice how you can no longer feel the B or P sounds on your hand.

Figure 28: A clip-on pop filter from £10

If you do use a pop filter, make sure to leave a gap between the filter and the mic - don't have it pressed up against the mic. Some mics include a pop filter, so check before you buy an additional one. Condenser mics are slightly more likely to benefit from a pop filter than dynamic ones but, given the low cost, it's probably worth getting a pop filter whatever mic you have - it can't really hurt, and can offset an unintentional movement towards a mic or help on a day when you seem to be talking about concepts that have more B, P and S sounds than usual. Additionally, a pop filter can protect against the accumulation of corrosive saliva on the microphone element which may improve the lifespan of the microphone.

Again, these types of sounds may not be noticeable to you, but mics respond differently than human ears - I found that mine was so sensitive that it could clearly pick up the sound of my carbonated drink fizzing if I placed the glass too close to it, even though the sound was almost imperceptible to me.

Shock mount

The final audio accessory to talk about is the shock mount. Again common in professional settings, these are meant to isolate microphones from physically transmitted noise - bumps and knocks against the desk or stand they're on, or even floor vibrations. Remember that, as well as picking up sounds in the air, mics will also amplify sounds from physical vibrations - if you bump the microphone (or the desk/stand it's on), drum your fingers on the table or just place a glass down, your audience may hear that noise much more clearly than you perceive it.

A shock mount suspends the microphone using elastic or plastic elastomers. Larger microphones tend to be more susceptible to environmental rumbles but unless there is some risk of external mechanical vibration in your particular setup, you're more likely to see audio improvements from other investments; shock mounts will yield little discernible difference in most domestic situations. As with pop filters, check to see if your chosen mic purchase includes a shock mount - a lot of bundles are available such as the "Yeticaster" which bundles the popular Yeti USB mic, boom arm and shock mount for £200. While many shock mounts are generic and fit common mics, you may need a specific solution if you've an unusual shaped mic like the Blue Snowball. If you don't have access to a formal shock mount, it's always worth experimenting with a layer of carpet, or even a towel placed under the feet of your mic stand's tripod legs. This should help to curtail the worst vibrations from reaching the mic.

Figure 29: An example of a shock mount

Testing

Whatever type of mic you choose, take plenty of time to test your microphone to ensure the best positioning. All of the main software packages for conferencing offer the ability to test your sound. Double check that you've selected the correct input if you've more than one mic - I've seen people buy expensive external mics but fail to switch the input from the other mic that's integrated into their webcam.

Record a short snippet in as typical a setup as possible. While the focus of listening in the previous chapter was on your voice delivery, this time, you need to appraise the sound quality. Experiment with different settings - for example, more gain will let you speak from further back but can increase background noise. If you notice your plosives popping, get a pop filter. If your kitchen table isn't as steady as you thought, consider a shock mount or a boom arm. If there's too much echo or ambient noise, try a sound shield. If you've gone the lavalier route, check carefully that your mounting isn't adding to the noise.

Audio Summary

Unless you're hoping to use the mic for music recording as well, around £50 is likely enough to get you a desktop USB mic that will strongly differentiate your sound quality from a built-in laptop mic. Any more than that may see diminishing returns for most ears but might bring extras like on-board gain/volume controls (as opposed to purely in the software) or switchable directional patterns that could be useful if you intend to use the mic beyond your presentations. Mics designated for podcast/game streaming are likely a good option for presenting too.

For more options on sound settings, refer to chapter 8 and the discussion of audio options that might be in your conferencing platform and could potentially duplicate or conflict with your microphone configuration.

As mentioned repeatedly in this book, a pragmatic approach is often preferable to a perfectionist one - if you think your lavalier mic is going to be visually distracting, it might be easier to buy a white one than try to hide a black one! Combinations of accessories may work best for your situation. If you've a noisy background and habit of tapping your foot, upgrading a Snowball mic with a shock mount and a shield might be better than buying a more expensive Yeti model. None of these accessories is going to compensate completely for the audio challenges compared to professional locations and equipment, but they may be useful to alleviate some issues. Even if they can't instantly turn a bad-sounding room into a perfect one, they may be able to provide your listeners with a clearer, smoother sound that better carries your message.

Chapter 7: Video and Camera

From a visual point of view, the pandemic has clearly exposed just how high the quality of video we're used to watching is - the production values on the TV shows we watch are stellar; the amateur videos from vloggers and even the smartphone uploads from teenagers on TikTok are beneficiaries from the amazing quality of the video cameras in today's affordable mobile devices. So, when we're faced with presenters with poorly lit, poorly framed feeds, from poor quality laptop webcams, they look particularly amateurish and unengaging.

Similarly to our discussion in the previous chapter about sound quality, how you look to your audience on video is a combination of your camera hardware, how you use it, and other environmental factors. Among the select winners from the overnight move to working from home, there's been an unprecedented rush on webcams, with virtually all leading models sold out and on back order. But before you rush to replace your integrated webcam (although that may be necessary), it's important to consider the totality of factors that contribute to the image your viewers will see - the combination of your lighting, framing and the camera hardware.

Fundamentals: Lighting, Framing and Hardware

I described in the previous chapter the lengths radio studios go to in order to maximise sound quality. In the same way, TV studios or professional video creators also obsess about their setup, especially with regard to lighting. Indeed, there are many parallels here to the previous chapter on microphones - ultimate performance is a combination of the hardware, environment and settings available to you and there's a range of upgrades and accessories that may suit some people, while others can significantly improve their video with just a few cost-free changes.

The camera is, of course, central to how your video looks, but it is also heavily influenced by positioning, framing and lighting. Just as you didn't need to be an audio technician in the previous chapter, we'll draw here on selected wisdom from cinematographers without distracting you from your focus on the content of your presentation.

Making improvements in and adaptations for your surroundings may well negate the need to spend money on more expensive hardware.

Regardless of the absolute quality of the camera at your disposal, there are things you can do to make the most visually of the equipment you have at your disposal. A good camera badly used can still yield off-putting or suboptimal video. Poor lighting or lazy framing, or how your shot is composed, can impact adversely on how the image looks to your viewers. Scenes that look effortless and natural usually have had the most planning put into them.

Framing and Composition

No matter what camera you're using, where it's positioned is a key determinant of what's in the frame and how it looks. There are two related considerations here: the position of the camera and your position within the frame. Camera framing refers to the position and placement of the subjects in your shots. Shots are all about composition - rather than pointing the camera in your general direction and hoping for the best, spend time explicitly to compose your image.

Camera Position

Before we move on to talk about external camera options, let's assume for now that you have a laptop. The first thing to do, whether you're planning on presenting from a sitting or standing position, is to raise your laptop so that your camera is at eye level. This free tip is one of the simplest and most effective ways to improve your online appearance. In the absence of a dedicated laptop stand, you can do this quickly by placing a box or a stack of books underneath your laptop. Make sure it's something sturdy so there's no danger of your laptop falling and invest in an extension cable if you need a longer power cord.

We tend to default to thinking in terms of laptop positioning for use when typing, so the ideal position for presenting may feel alien and may indeed be unsuitable for work use but you need to think a bit creatively about how you make the most of your laptop for this new task you're asking of it. And then move it back to a more agreeable working position when you are back to deskwork.

Laptops generally need to be raised up to offer a good perspective from their integrated cameras but few people take the effort to adjust the position from normal - this is partly why so many remote appearances on TV during the pandemic don't look right - we're so used to well framed camerawork from cameras at the correct height that laptops on a desk looking up at the presenter seem jarring to the audience. The lack of an eye level perspective gives a subconscious feeling that the presenter is looking down on us. Having the camera looking up at a person can make them appear more imposing, whereas appearing to look down at a person can diminish them.

The Eyes Have It

Once you have your camera at the right height, don't forget to look at it! The natural temptation is to just look at your screen, below the camera, where the slides are. But that gives you an odd, distracted look that subtly tells the other party something interests you more than them. Of course, you'll look away from the camera to consult what's on your screen from time to time, but try to maintain regular eye contact with the camera, especially when you're talking. As you can see below, I've printed out a little arrow that I attach to the top of my camera to make sure I never forget! It's likely this won't be necessary for much longer - check out the section in chapter 8 that discusses an AI-based solution to eye contact.

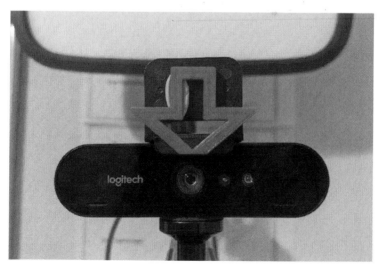

Figure 30: I've printed a little arrow to remind me to look at the camera

In video production, there's a long-established composition guideline called 'the rule of thirds'. Imagine the screen split up in thirds both vertically and horizontally. Things positioned along the intersection of the lines have a good chance of "looking right".

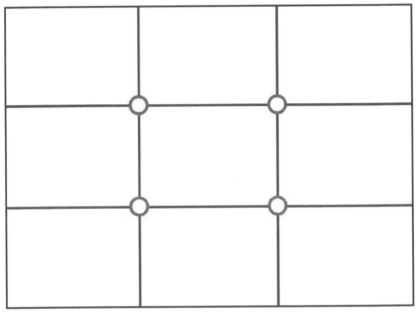

Figure 31: The Rule of Thirds

Try to position your eyes roughly along the top line. That should ensure about the right amount of "headroom" or space between the top of your head and top of the frame. If in doubt, leave a little bit more rather than less headroom to account for the image getting cropped en route to your audience. Unless there's a reason to sit or stand off centre (such as something in the background, you should be in the middle of the frame, or the empty space will look strange.

Framing creates an emotion in the viewer - the wrong angle can cause a sense of claustrophobia or intimidation - shots with too little headroom look wrong, giving a subtle cramped sense - framing with your face at eye-level creates a sense of equality. For most presentations, the rules of framing are fairly consistent - framing may vary for advanced setups such as the software called 'mmhmm' discussed in chapter 9.

As you consider your shot choice, remember that domestically produced webinars remove many of the tools that TV and filmmakers use to keep us engaged - there's typically no change of shot as you present. For contrast, now watch a TV show and count how long before any shot changes....the average is around 5 seconds, and just 2.5 seconds in commercials. The lack of variety in shots in typical online presentations from home makes it especially critical to choose the right one, and to push your content to work harder and provide visual stimulus and variety as discussed in chapter 2.

Shot Choice

Your choice of shot should be an explicit, conscious decision, not a by-product of where your laptop happens to be, or where your chair is usually positioned. There are entire books about framing and composition alone, but here I'll just highlight some norms that will quickly make your video look better.

Key to how you're perceived on screen is how much of you is visible. Cinematographers will carefully choose shots (see the diagram for the range of shots overleaf) and move between different shots as appropriate. In most online presenting situations however, you will be restricted to a single shot. For seated presentations, this should be a medium close up (MCU) shot, while for standing, a medium shot (MS) is most normal. Avoid closeup and big close up that people get with laptop webcams - this is not a natural shot choice; it's unsettling and intimidating for the viewer and restrictive for the presenter who is trying to stay in a shot that rules out any form of visible gestures to bring more life to the presentation.

Continuing with what I said above about positioning your laptop for the best camera height rather than its normal desktop position, if you are sitting when presenting, you should consider whether it's possible to sit further back than you normally would. As laptops have become more compact, it means the camera can end up being very close to the user, which means your face nearly fills the frame - that's not a view that we're comfortable with; it's rarely used on professional TV or film other than for brief periods of emphasis. As an experiment, watch some TV critically and you'll notice that the people are almost always framed at more distance - they are rarely sitting as close to the camera as we do with a laptop - so that's a much more natural-looking arrangement for viewers.

Remember that's what you're competing with or being judged against. This is how people are conditioned to consume media on their screens and when you deviate from it, the result doesn't look as good to the viewer. Compare the shots illustrated below and consider how you look on your webcam and then compare how a professionally-produced web presentation from a TED talk looks.

Of course, moving back from the laptop may be a challenge if you're reliant on its integrated mic. This probably helps to justify using a USB desktop microphone that you can place between you and the laptop, bringing the microphone closer to you while maintaining a better distance for the camera.

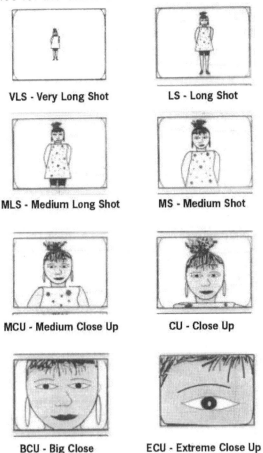

Figure 32: Standard camera shots - there are way too many BCUs happening on webcams!

Having a visible mic in frame isn't something we're used to in most professional broadcasts as broadcasters go to great lengths to hide mics, as discussed in the previous chapter. But in domestic situations, I think it's more than acceptable. It may even show your audience that you've taken additional steps to ensure a good experience for them.

Hand Gestures

I recommended earlier that you continue to make natural hand gestures when presenting, as this aids your voice projection. From a visual point of view, keep in mind that you may need to hold your hands slightly higher than you normally would to keep them visible in the frame, depending on your shot choice - consider an MS instead of an MCU - but even if they're not visible, don't stop moving your hands as you'll seem wooden otherwise.

Distractions

Returning to the topic of distractions, try to make sure that you've minimised visual distractions as well as audible ones. For example, I've noticed that my eyes are involuntarily drawn to motion outside - so if possible, it's preferable to pick a room that doesn't overlook the street. Remember that you're on camera the whole time, so try not to get distracted or do anything that might distract other people in the video conference. Don't try to multitask, checking your phone or emails, don't fidget or roll around if your chair has wheels.

Background

Of course, once you've got yourself perfectly positioned in the shot, a key part of your composition - and potential distraction for your audience - is what's going on behind you. Basic composition rules apply - don't have things growing out of your head or have bright distractions behind you. Ideally, don't have too much depth in the background as that will draw the viewers' eyes. Depending on your technical capabilities, you'll usually have a choice of either finding a neutral background or displaying a virtual background to mask what is actually behind you. Virtual backgrounds can be fully computer-imposed, or some platforms may require the use of a green screen and a technique known as chromakey (more on that below).

Real Backgrounds

Your goal for a background should be to minimise any visual clutter behind you - plain is good. Not necessarily plain to the point of eliminating all personality, but it's more professional if people aren't straining to identify objects behind you, distracted by the corner of a piece of art or trying to discern what books are on your shelves. Non-distracting backgrounds, with no moving parts, no clocks and no screens work best.

Blur or Virtual

Manipulating your background with software is a relatively new capability but is increasingly common across the major conferencing and collaboration platforms. The most basic approach is to blur your real background to remove any distractions. I quite like the blur effect - it tends to be less distracting than the full virtual background, but offers no opportunity for branding.

As you decide on a background strategy though, beware of the strain it can place on your computer - generating a virtual background is very computationally intensive and can cause noticeable slowdowns of lower-power computers, or provoke significant fan noise. Despite meeting the minimum specifications, my laptop fan switches on after just a few minutes of virtual background use. Next time around, I'll opt for a more powerful processor or a fanless laptop. Zoom provides an up-to-date list of system requirements for software-generated virtual backgrounds on its website[7].

Also, avoid the temptation to use fancy video backgrounds (instead of still images) as they are too distracting in a formal context, unless you're opting for your slides as a background. If your computer is powerful enough, Zoom supports sharing your slides as a virtual background - this can be a useful option if you want to be more visible than other views allow. But it does require additional consideration of your slide layout - though you can move where you appear and the size your image is overlaid, as shown below.

---

[7]https://support.zoom.us/hc/en-us/articles/360043484511-System-requirements-for-Virtual-Background

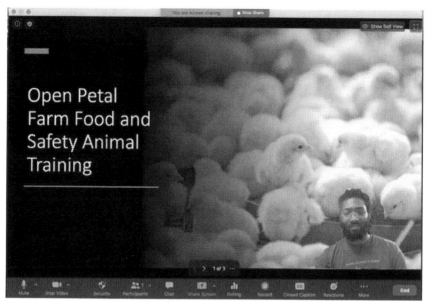

Figure 33: An MCU view of the presenter super-imposed in the bottom right corner over the background of slides. Image courtesy of Zoom

To use this feature, you must have either PowerPoint or Keynote installed locally on your device, so Google Slides is out. It also allows you to manage your presentation directly from within the Zoom meeting controls. Note though, that sound, transitions, or animations embedded in slides are not supported. If your system and confidence are up to this style of presentation, make sure the presentation is still about your content and not about you!

If you're using a platform that doesn't have the virtual background feature available to you, there are third party services you can investigate such as:

- XSplit Vcam ($50 lifetime license or $6/month)
- ManyCam ($60/year for virtual backgrounds)
- Chromacam.me ($30)

These products are quite easy to use and require only minimal configuration, so are worth a try if you need a virtual background.

91

Green Screen

Since long before software was powerful enough to dynamically replace backgrounds, green screens have been a mainstay of TV studios and movie special effects. And despite the fact that some home computers can use software to simulate a virtual background, lower-power computers and more professional results require the use of a green screen and a technique called 'chromakey' that replaces the solid colour with your chosen image.

The use of a solid colour behind you provided by the screen is easy for the platform to identify and is more accurate than its software estimation of where you end and the background begins, so a green screen gives a sharper image than virtual background replacement. Although referred to generically as green screen, you can also use other solid colours such as blue screens. For example, if you're wearing green, then you'll need a blue screen to avoid merging into the background!

Depending on how permanent your home office setup is, you can choose from a wall or ceiling-mounted screen that you pull down like a blind, or a more portable pull-up stand. There are even chair-mounted options for those with less space.

Figure 34: (L) A chair-mount green screen and (R) pop-up version (about 70 inches/180cm tall)

Camera Terminology

Now that we've discussed some basics around how best to position yourself and your camera for good video, it's time to cover the actual camera hardware options in more detail.

When assessing webcams for use in your presentations, there are usually three main technology specifications to consider: resolution, frame rate and field of view (FOV). Clearer images have a higher resolution, and a higher frame rate means that movements appear smoother on the screen. The larger the field of view, the wider the shot; the narrower the field of view, the more zoomed in the image.

Resolution

As you might know from shopping for a TV, image resolution is measured by the number of pixels on the screen, measured length by width. The three most common resolutions are:

- Standard high definition - HD Ready or 720p
- Full high definition - FHD or 1080p
- Ultra-high definition - UHD or 4K

Most live video streamed over Zoom and other conferencing or collaboration platforms is at 720p resolution as that's the most common resolution for integrated webcams, as well as offering a reasonable mix between image quality and not requiring too much bandwidth. Refer back to the table in chapter 5 about how much bandwidth varies by resolution.

However, there is a noticeable improvement in video quality if you use a Full-HD camera at 1080p. Although budget webcams sometimes only offer 720p, 1080p webcams are now available for around £20, only a £5 premium over 720p models. There is a limited number of 4K webcams available - these are capable of producing much higher quality video, but result in file sizes that require a lot of bandwidth. Although marketing has programmed consumers always to look for more resolution or megapixels, there is no need for 4K webcams for most situations. It will place unnecessary strain on your laptop and your internet connection, for an audience that is most likely not viewing you on a 4K screen or a screen large enough to benefit from ultra-high resolution. 4K webcams are unlikely to be necessary for live events but may be useful if you want to record and edit footage and make it available as a UHD download. Note that 4K webcams can be set to stream at 1080 or 720 as required.

Frame Rate

The other key metric for perceived video quality is frame rate, which specifies how many still images (frames) comprise a video file. Measured in frames per second (fps), the higher the frame rate, the smoother looking the video will be, though the resulting stream may be quite large in size, especially if each frame is high resolution (see above). The minimum frame rate for acceptable video is 15 fps, but 30 or 60 fps will look more natural, with less 'flicker'. A camera may only be able to capture high frame rates at lower resolutions; for example, a camera may capture 60fps at 720p, but only be able to capture 30fps at full 1080p.

Given the overall constraint of wishing to keep file sizes small enough to stream easily, different use cases may choose different combinations of frame rate and resolution. For example, if your stream includes fast moving sequences - such as a video game clip - you might opt for 720p at 60fps, whereas if the ultimate quality of the video is more important and there's no fast movement in the shot, you would choose 1080p at 30fps. The default setting on most webcams of 720p at 30fps is usually fine for presentations.

Field of View

Another specification to look out for on webcams, which isn't directly related to quality in the way resolution and frame rate are, is the 'field of view' - a webcam's field of view (FOV) refers to the width of the area that it can capture. A webcam with a wide-angle lens has broader field of view; in the product specifications, you will find FOV measured in degrees:

- 60-degrees captures one person sitting in front of a computer.
- 78-degrees is wide enough to capture two people facing a camera mounted to a computer monitor.
- 90-degrees is great for showing a whiteboard or a group of people seated at a conference room table.

The more expensive webcam models may offer variable fields of view but consider your environment - if you're stuck for space, a narrower field of view that shows less of your home may be more desirable than a wide view.

With those technical details covered, let's assess the options - from making the most of integrated cameras and popular external webcams to using your phone or a DSLR. Today, many camera options offer near broadcast quality video, so it can be very much a matter of personal preference and budget in deciding about what's best for your set up.

Integrated Webcams

For laptop users, the starting point is nearly always an integrated camera, usually in the top edge of the lid. Desktop computer users have probably already had to invest in a USB webcam that's clipped atop their monitor. Much like the integrated microphones that tend not to be high quality, we're rapidly discovering that integrated webcams are another area where manufacturers have cut corners, on the assumption we wouldn't use them extensively. Integrated webcams also offer severely limited mobility - raising an entire laptop device to a better camera view height is much harder than positioning an external camera device at eye level.

If you recall for a moment how as our phones became thinner over the last few years, all the top models now sport a camera bump - proof that shrinking a camera module isn't always possible or desirable when image quality is important. Yet the lid on my MacBook Air is a fraction of the depth of my iPhone 11, which infers that the integrated camera is compromised; the tiny space allotted to the webcam in the laptop lid leaves little room for large sensors or quality lens components. The lack of emphasis on webcam evolution can be seen in the fact that the MacBook camera hardware hasn't been updated since the introduction of 720p models in 2012 - ironically you can find a better front-facing camera on a £200 phone than on a £2,000 laptop.

Figure 35: A MacBook's camera module in front of an external webcam

In fairness, although they have been an under-developed component, integrated webcams can offer reasonable results given the right steps to optimise conditions.

Position

The default angle between your face and your laptop on a desk is not ideal for creating a flattering or attentive look, and there's not much you can do about it when the webcam is fixed inside a laptop screen. If you can't elevate the laptop, then definitely don't sit with it on your lap. The motion will drive your audience crazy as it will amplify your tiniest unconscious movement, while the angle will be very unflattering! So, as described above, sit back. Sit further back from your laptop than your instinct tells you!

External Webcam

Just like upgrading your microphone, an external camera is a key consideration to improve your presentation quality. Aside from the likelihood it will offer a significant upgrade over the capabilities of your integrated camera, it gives significant positioning flexibility and releases you from being tied to a seated position in front of the laptop. Although many webcams offer clips to mount on the top of the laptop lid, they also tend to come with a tripod mount, which means you can position them on a tripod or use a goose-neck mount to move them closer to eye level.

Since their design is not dictated by the space constraints of a laptop lid, external webcams typically have higher quality components, including a larger sensor and multi piece lens providing for better resolution, colour balance, low light performance and field of view.

We'll talk more about the importance of lighting later in this chapter, but note that some webcams offer basic integrated lighting which can save you the cost of an external light and also offers a space saving. The Razer Kiyo camera is a popular high resolution choice that includes integrated lighting, while more complex units such as the Marantz AVS offer more height (it stands 48cm/18" tall) than an integrated laptop camera, as well as an integrated ring light with colour filters.

Figure 36: External webcams may include integrated lighting: (L) Razer Kiyo and (R) Marantz AVS

Wireless Webcam

For the ultimate in positional flexibility, streaming camera supplier Mevo is working on upgrades to its wireless camera to make it function as a webcam, but the £400 price point places it firmly above the price of even the most expensive wired webcams (the 4K Logitech Brio at £200 is already twice the price of many good HD models).

Other Features

With wired webcam prices ranging from £20 to £200, despite seemingly similar resolution and frame rates, choosing the right model for your needs may be as simple as deciding which design fits best in your setup or there may be a specific feature that appeals to you. Also consider if there's an accessory that will turn your existing mid-range webcam into everything you need - a simple gooseneck extension may solve your mounting problems and get your camera to that all-important eye level.

Integrated microphones

Many external webcams also include microphones alongside their camera capabilities. These are unlikely to be as good as dedicated microphones, but they are still usually better than the integrated laptop ones, with the benefit of a single connection and taking up less space. Be aware, though, of the contradictory advice to back away from the camera but get close to your microphone! Make sure you're familiar with your conferencing software settings for selecting the intended microphone and camera inputs when you connect your external webcam/microphones.

Software Setup/Management

Adding an external webcam to your setup is usually very easy. Almost all web cams come with a USB connection, and thanks to a standard called UVC (USB-Video Class), the cameras are compatible with all common software, without the need for any additional drivers or setup. The new camera will just appear in your settings as available for use in Zoom, Teams or other software. Many better webcams also have software-controlled features for manually fine-tuning settings such as brightness, contrast, colour intensity, and white balance. If you're investing in an expensive external webcam, take the additional time to understand and optimise these settings, but most external webcams require no configuration.

Popular Webcams

When assessing your webcam needs, remember that the intended target market for the camera's features will influence the price point. Make sure you buy according to your requirements - just as with microphones, buying the most expensive, on the assumption it's the best, isn't correct in all contexts. Webcams aimed at game streamers, for example, will likely include high frame rate modes that are unnecessary for a sedate presentation.

Here's some examples of popular external model specifications:

	Entry	**Mid**	**High**	**Ultra**
Brand	Logitech		Razer	Logitech
Model	C270	C920	Kiyo	Brio
Price (Typical, £)	35	80	100	200
Resolution	720	1080	1080	4K
Frame Rate	30	30	30/60	Up to 90
FOV	60	78	81.6	65-78-90
Focus	Fixed	Auto	Auto	Auto
Lens	Plastic	Glass	Glass	Glass
Microphone	Mono	Stereo	Omni	Omni
Lighting	-	-	Ring	-

Phone as Webcam

Another option to improve the quality of your video is to use what is probably the best quality camera device in many households - a good smartphone. And there's the added benefit that if you're using it as your camera, you won't be tempted to check your messages during the presentation!

Your options when it comes to using your phone as a webcam will vary based on the phone model you have but in general, you will need to add some additional software on your phone, and probably on your laptop too. There are plenty of competing apps - note that some only offer limited free versions and you'll have to pay to unlock all features. Use the free version to test if it all works before paying for the full version. I've tried Elgato Epoccam (£8) on iOS and Droidcam on Android (£5) and the quality is excellent if you've a good phone. The Wi-Fi connection to your laptop is convenient and again, remember to select the correct inputs in your conferencing software.

Figure 37: Mount your smartphone at eye level as an alternative webcam

Keep in mind if you do opt to use your phone, that you'll need to mount it appropriately, which may require buying a tripod or gooseneck and a holder that fits your device. Consider also what you plan to do for sound when using the phone as a webcam - your phone's microphone is designed for very close use and may not respond well if you're any distance from it. Wired options are diminishing as many phones no longer have 3.5mm jacks. There are microphones available with USB-C and Lighting connectors for phones, but I'd expect to see more Bluetooth options in the near future. Of course, you can use your phone as a webcam and use a separate desktop or lavalier microphone connected to your laptop as long as you select the different video and audio sources in your settings and check they aren't out of sync.

Using a phone camera also brings us back to the framing challenge - phones are largely designed for use in portrait or upright mode, whereas TVs/monitors and DSLRs are usually landscape. Plan to mount the phone horizontally - vertical video doesn't look good for presenting as it has too much headroom and is too narrow on your audience's screens, which forces the video conferencing software to put black bars on the sides of the image.

DSLR as Webcam

While most people present themselves to the world via a tiny cheap camera stuffed into the slim lid of their laptop and don't consider using their smartphone camera, in many homes there is another, far superior camera that only comes out for vacations and special occasions. Given that there were over 8.6 million DSLRs sold worldwide in 2019 alone[8], lots of households have access to very high-quality digital cameras. It's a shame to see a £500 or £1000 DSLR sit unused as you broadcast via a £10 integrated camera module. (While I'm talking about DSLRs, many recent camcorders, mirrorless, bridge, compact and action cameras can also be used as webcams - Google your model).

Like other types of camera, you need to ensure good positioning of your DSLR - all cameras have a tripod mount, but make sure your tripod is especially steady if you're placing the camera at eye level, higher than you might for a portrait. You should connect it to power as DSLR batteries tend not to last long when recording video. As discussed above for smartphones, you also may want to look into recording your audio with a separate microphone rather than the in-camera mic if you want the best sound, but again a reminder that DSLR mic connectors tend to be different than smartphones - so double check your TRS and TRRS leads from chapter 6.

[8]https://petapixel.com/2020/09/18/heres-how-many-dslrs-and-mirrorless-cameras-top-brands-shipped-in-2019/

DSLRs were designed to be very good at taking photos and at recording video, but weren't originally intended to act as stationary video cameras for streaming a presentation. There are a couple of different ways to actually turn your DSLR into a webcam depending on your camera, whether it has USB or HDMI output, and if you're connecting to a PC or Mac.

If your camera only has a HDMI output, you'll need some additional hardware to convert it to USB for input to your computer. Although most modern computers have HDMI ports, they are only for output - connecting to a monitor - and can't accept a video input. I've used the Elgato Cam Link 4K (£100), compatible with most cameras, which takes the HDMI output from your camera, plugs into your laptop via USB and appears to the computer as a webcam input.

Figure 38: A HDMI to USB device can connect any camera with clean HDMI output to your computer

2020 has seen a rush of DSLR vendors releasing software connectivity options. Canon, Nikon, Sony and Fuji, for example, have all released updates of varying degrees of completeness. Google your camera model to see what the best options are, as well as details of what cables you might require.

Lighting

The single factor that can give even a low-cost camera a big step up in performance is your lighting. If you have control over your lighting, you can mitigate many shortcomings of a camera and produce a much higher quality video feed. Putting some effort into your lighting setup can be enough to overcome many of the shortcomings of integrated cameras, meaning you may not need to invest in an upgrade; even if you have a more expensive camera, improved lighting is still key to extracting maximum performance from the device.

When you're assessing your surroundings for a suitably-lit location, there are a few basic caveats - avoid sitting with a window behind you and the camera in front of you. Unlike human eyes, cameras struggle with scenes of large contrast and the auto exposure settings on your camera will try to even out the lighting between you and the bright background of the window, which can lead to your face being overly dark. You should also try to ensure the camera isn't pointed at any direct sources of light - this can be tricky if you have ceiling spotlights - try to point them away from the camera if you have adjustable downlights. And remember that natural light sources change - whether weather-related or time of day - so keep that in mind if you're working across time zones - I've done rehearsals for presentations in broad daylight with ideal bright natural light which is very different as you deliver live at 3am to an audience on the other side of the globe.

Domestic Lights

Most domestic setups are not lit for high quality broadcast video - domestic lighting isn't typically designed for careful control of lighting on a single spot where a presenter is positioned. A defining factor in TV studio design is the flexibility of lighting, allowing it to be moved and controlled in terms of direction, intensity and colour temperature. When you're assessing your lighting options, remember that the human eye has a remarkable ability to adjust for light conditions - don't trust your visual impression of how well or badly a position is lit - check how the camera you will be using sees it.

Remember also that cameras perceive colour temperature more clearly than humans - domestic lighting may appear more orange to a camera than it does to a human. Although we can tell warm light (orange) from cold light (blue), our eyes tend to adjust, and we don't notice unless the light is very harsh or very warm.

In domestic situations, the most common source of lighting is overhead bulbs. While these may be diffused by a light fitting, overhead lighting is not flattering on camera - if you've ever had a professional portrait taken, you'll have noticed the use of "fill" lights at head height. This is to reduce the harsh shadows under eyes, nose and cheeks that you get from overhead-only lighting. To compensate for the shadow-generating overhead lights, if possible, try to add a light source coming from at, or slightly above, eye-level. This will depend if you're sitting or standing, but a lampstand can be repurposed if there's one available in the house.

Depending on the orientation of your presentation space, an ideal non-overhead source can be for the presenter to face a window (not with too direct sunlight) as this will give a flattering soft light. In the absence of this, see if you can perhaps face a plain pale wall and setup a desk lamp with the light bouncing off the wall. This will give a soft flattering even light. Standing for your presentation will probably introduce additional lighting challenges, but you may be able to repurpose a lamp to provide head level fill lighting from out of shot.

If your only option is to sit with a window behind you, then you'll need to give strong consideration to a more powerful fill light solution of some sort. If you think your lighting is ok and you still look too warm (orange) or too cold (white/blue), check your camera's white balance setting. Look at whites in your shot like a shirt, teeth or eyes and check how white they look.

Mini Fill Lights/Ring

If you're sitting, there is now a range of small but powerful mini lamps you can quickly attach to the top of your laptop or position on a desktop tripod to provide semi-professional levels of controlled lighting. Most will offer colour temperature control so you can choose from a warm or cool light depending on your decor, pallor and how your camera handles exposure.

Figure 39: (L) Desk-mounted lights start at around £50 while Ring lights (R) start at about £15

With the growth in selfie culture and especially make-up videos on social media, there is also a wide range of ring lights available at very low cost. These provide a shadow-free and even light, that also adds a nice effect to your eyes. Several of the models of ring lights also come with filters to adjust the light temperature.

Key Lights

If you have the luxury of budget and space, there are more advanced options available that will offer greater control over lighting, but are definitely on the overkill end for many people. A popular solution among gaming streamers and vloggers is the Elgato Light. Though not cheap, it offers remote control via an app or Stream Deck (more on that later) and a mounting system that can accommodate an eye level camera and a microphone. *Disclosure - this is my personal setup.*

Figure 40: The Elgato Key Light and Multimount - probably only justified for semi-professional presenters (£200)

Video Summary

Just as better microphones bring challenges around increased sensitivity not only to your voice but to extraneous sounds, better cameras have their own challenges. Upgrading your camera may force you to pay more attention to your lighting, as well as placing additional strain on your computer. In return though, you'll appear much clearer and smoother to your viewers.

Chapter 8: Software

When you've adapted your content, practiced, optimised your environment and carefully positioned your camera and microphone, the final stage of the journey to improved online presenting is to ensure you've mastered the software that brings it all together into a coherent experience for your audience.

It used to be sufficient to gain proficiency in your presentation app of choice - usually Keynote, PowerPoint or Google slides - to deliver your content. Virtual presenting adds at least one additional layer of complexity and you need to be sure you're familiar with the settings and options for the platform you're presenting on - typically Zoom, Google Meet or Microsoft Teams, though there are many other alternatives available.

In this section, I'll primarily use Zoom (as at late 2020) to illustrate the examples, but these may be slightly different in other tools and are subject to change as Zoom updates its offering regularly to add new features. Note if some Zoom options mentioned are not available on your setup, it may be that your computer isn't powerful enough - Zoom hides options if your device doesn't meet the minimum specifications. The key thing is to check the options available in your chosen platform and ensure you're fully familiar with the features.

Alongside your presentation software and the core video conferencing platforms, there are several other pieces of additional software that may address a particular need, as you seek to improve your performance. Also, if you choose to use some of the accessories mentioned here, you may require specific software to configure or control these. With any software you do end up using, I strongly advise exploring all the settings available to ensure you're making the most of your investments - many products lead on ease of use but also provide myriad features under "Advanced Settings" that you may benefit from customising. Don't be afraid to experiment during your practice time to see what combination of settings suits your setup best.

Accessibility Features

A positive feature of the increase in online presentations is that it can significantly improve accessibility to events for people with challenges or disabilities. Not only can your presentation reach more people who may not have had the chance to attend a real-life presentation, many presentation software platforms now offer extensive and impressive accessibility tools. Ensure you consider how to maximise accessibility and discuss this in advance with your host/organizer.

As a presenter, you should ensure that materials you create offer maximum accessibility. Refer to the Web Accessibility Initiative for more guidance on this important area:
https://www.w3.org/WAI/teach-advocate/accessible-presentations/

All the major conferencing platforms offer free accessibility features that you should take time to be familiar with including:

- Closed Captioning
- Automated Transcription
- Ability to pin an interpreter webcam (if present) alongside the speaker

So Many Settings

If you typically give presentations to internal audiences in your organisation, you will probably have only one platform to use regularly as dictated by your IT infrastructure. If you are a professional speaker, you will likely need to be comfortable with a variety of online platforms too. While Zoom is often spoken of as the major winner in the pandemic, Microsoft Teams has grown dramatically, while Google Meet has also been aggressively promoted and had features added. Some organisations use older platforms such as WebEx, while yet more have turned to new offerings such as Hopin. Most software platforms offer a similar set of core features, but can label and locate them differently, so it's always important to make sure you're comfortable well in advance of giving a presentation. If the organiser of the event you're speaking to doesn't proactively offer, make sure you ask for access to test and familiarise yourself if the platform is new to you.

Many presenters I've spoken to have a tendency to join online sessions and be so pleased that it works at all, that they largely ignore the available settings and preferences. However, the defaults are not always ideal and, in some cases, can conflict with your efforts to improve; the standard settings are designed for lowest common denominator situations. For example, prominent microphone vendor, Samson, advises against using the default audio configuration on Zoom[9].

In the next few sections, I'll look at some of the more common types of settings you may encounter as you explore the capabilities and vagaries of these platforms.

Audio Settings

Zoom offers several settings that are intended to improve the audio experience, especially for people who may be joining from poor quality setups. The Zoom app has options to configure its noise suppression features, which are designed to help remove distracting noises that can be picked up by participants' microphones. Background noises, such as typing, paper rustling on the desk, fan noise from the computer or AC, dogs barking, and other noises will be filtered out to reduce audio distractions. By default, on Zoom this feature is enabled, however the option can be changed to be more or less aggressive, based on the environment and use case.

---

[9] https://blog.samson.co/blog/2020/04/setting-up-your-samson-usb-mic-with-zoom-conferencing/

Figure 41: Zoom Audio Settings

The following options are available:

- Auto: This is the default setting and will apply moderate background noise reduction when needed. It will auto adjust the aggressiveness for blocking background noise based on what it detects in the background. If music is detected, it will not treat the music as background noise.
- Low: Noise reduction will be minimal. It will only remove low levels of persistent background noise. This setting is best for casually playing music, as it will preserve as much of the original sound as possible. For highest fidelity when playing music, consider using the Enable Original Audio setting in your advanced audio settings (see below).
- Medium: Best for reducing and eliminating background noise in standard environments, including fans, pen tapping, etc.
- High: Noise reduction will be at its most aggressive, and eliminate noise such as crunching of paper or wrappers, keyboard typing, etc. Note: Enabling this option may increase CPU utilization.

Zoom also offers the ability to turn off all its audio filtering features and use the direct sound from your microphone. The setting "Original sound" allows you to preserve the sound from your microphone without using Zoom's echo cancellation and audio-enhancing features. This is ideal if your microphone or sound equipment has these features built-in and you do not need the

110

additional enhancement. In fact, multiple competing noise filtering systems can degrade the quality rather than enhance it.

If you find Zoom's noise reduction features don't work for your noise issues, Krisp (https://krisp.ai) is an app that acts as a virtual microphone. It uses AI to filter out unwanted noise. If you install Krisp, you need to select it as your microphone in your conferencing platform settings for its filters to be applied. As you evolve your setup and possibly change your hardware, it's worth trying different settings to see what delivers the best result.

Video Settings

Zoom also offers several settings that attempt to improve video quality. Just below the setting to choose which camera to use (essential if you've an external webcam to select instead of your laptop's default internal cam), are a couple of options Zoom provides where its software will try to improve your video before viewers see you.

There's a variable "touch up my appearance" option, as well as a binary setting to add adjustment for low light. Try both of these to see if they improve your video feed, but keep in mind that actual lighting improvements are likely to give better results than the adjust for low light setting.

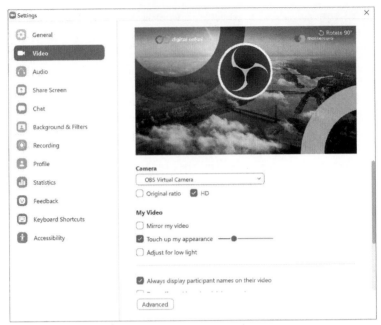

Figure 42: Zoom Video Settings

Hardware settings

Depending on the hardware you've added to your setup, it may provide additional software to control specific settings. For example, here's the configuration app that comes with the Logitech Brio Webcam:

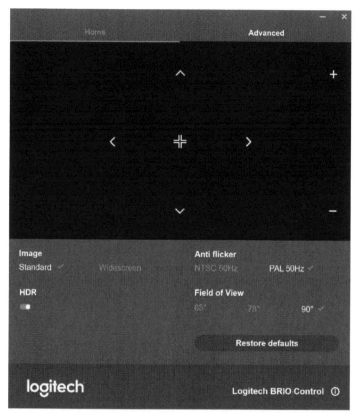
Figure 43: Logitech Brio Camera Settings App

Screen Sharing

Most conferencing systems give control over who can share to the meeting 'host' - so ensure in advance that the host has given you permission to share your screen - it's annoying for participants if the host announces you're about to present and the next thing they hear is you having to say "I don't have screen sharing permission" and the host then scrabbling to find the option to give you the additional privileges.

Views

Most presentation packages have a number of different views or screen layouts available to help presenters. This includes the ability to show a different view to you as presenter compared to the slide output that the audience sees. This is extremely handy for seeing what slide is coming next, as well as speaker notes and additional information such as a timer. This is the key reason why I recommended adding a second monitor when discussing the basic computing setup back in chapter 5.

Presenter View

Presenter View (available in PowerPoint and Google Slides) allows you to privately display your current slide, your next slide, your Speaker Notes, and a storyboard of future slides. You also get a prominent clock and timer to stay on point. Having a preview of your next slide is invaluable as it allows you to move between slides smoothly rather than the less-than-professional surprised pause when the next slide appears and you adjust to it.

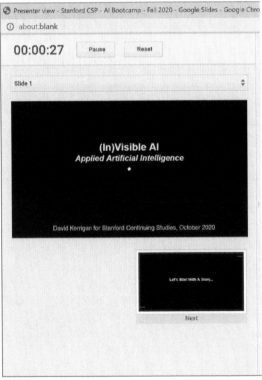

Figure 44: Presenter View in Google Slides - use this view on a second screen as it lets you (and not the audience) preview what's next so you can smoothly introduce the content

Future Views

There's little doubt that the dramatic shift to online conferencing in 2020 will see rapid innovation in the capabilities of the software involved. Already in mid-2020, Microsoft announced a new feature for Teams called Teams Together which tries to recreate a more room-like view using AI to isolate participant's video and superimpose them to make it look like they're in a single room. Although early, I'd expect to see a variety of experiments and innovations as tech firms try to differentiate their experiences.

Figure 45: Microsoft Teams view as an alternative to a gallery of faces in boxes

I'll finish this section with a further example of the coming innovation in this space. Remember my emphasis in chapter 6 on the importance of eye contact and looking at the camera as opposed to the screen? Well, an experimental feature from Microsoft may offer a resolution for this quandary: an AI system that subtly adjusts your video to make it look like you're looking directly at the camera! Currently only available on one model of Surface computer[10], this will surely come to more devices and platforms if it proves popular.

---

[10]https://blogs.windows.com/devices/2020/08/20/make-a-more-personal-connection-with-eye-contact-now-generally-available/

Figure 46: Microsoft experimental feature to alter the video to make it look like you're looking at the camera if you look down at the screen - see how the eyes on the right image have been adjusted to make it look like the presenter is looking at the audience directly.

Chapter 9: Advanced Options

Once you've mastered the basics, if you want to take your presentations to the next level, there are further options to consider. But beware that these add complexity and shouldn't be considered until you're completely comfortable with the core tools and techniques. Additional complexity can look impressive when it works, but if you over-reach, you'll end up looking less competent rather than more!

Non-professional presenters are unlikely to need the options discussed in this chapter as they cater to specific situations, where you need to include multiple camera sources, to deliver complex scripts, interact with the audience or want to control a number of accessories. With the exception of the rehearsal software, if you don't absolutely need one of the features discussed in this chapter, I'd strongly recommend focusing instead on the quality of your content and nailing the basics around lighting, sound and video.

Practice Software aids

You'll probably have gathered I'm a big advocate of practice but being self-aware and self-critical isn't easy. After you've bugged your family/ trusted colleagues/friends to critique your work, you can turn to some artificial intelligence for further feedback. The apps discussed below predate the growth in online presenting but the basic principles of presenting apply.

PowerPoint Coach

Available in Microsoft's popular PowerPoint software, this tool gives you real-time feedback on your pacing, for example, tells you whether you are using inclusive language and how many filler words you use. It also makes sure that you don't commit the greatest sin of presenting: just reading the slides.

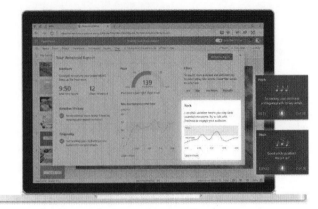

Figure 47: Microsoft PowerPoint offers a coaching mode

Orai

One of the more popular presentation coaching apps out there, Orai, uses AI to analyse your speech and provide feedback on aspects such as clarity, use of filler words, pace, and vocal energy to identify areas for improvement. It can also use your smartphone camera to assess your facial expressions. Free trial with a $10 monthly fee thereafter.

Figure 48: Orai is one of several apps that listen to you practice and provide coaching feedback

Virtual Reality for Offline Presenting

If you're new to presenting during the pandemic and want help getting ready to go back to real conference rooms, there are impressive VR training apps now to help prepare you for large audiences. With affordable VR hardware like the Oculus Quest 2 starting at €349, I'm sure we'll see Learning & Development departments in firms looking to make these available to staff keen to prepare for the transition from online presenting back to auditoria.

Figure 49: VR Training for presenting offline. Image Courtesy VirtualSpeech.com

mmhmm

Perhaps the most unusually named software of 2020, mmhmm's creators claim they wanted to have a product whose name is easily pronounced when your mouth is full! Aiming to bring a degree of creative flexibility when presenting, mmhmm allows you to add a variety of effects without requiring particularly high specification hardware.

It also allows you to superimpose yourself over slides and add virtual backgrounds.

Figure 50: mmhmm lets you point to your slides as you present

While it can definitely relieve the monotony of a webinar presentation, it can also look a bit distracting and gimmicky, so use it sparingly and make sure to practice thoroughly before using it in a live presentation. As of late November 2020, mmhmm is only available on Mac, with Windows support promised soon. mmhmm is $10/month, though you can use it for an hour a day for free.

Stream Deck

While you're presenting it can be quite distracting and slightly impractical to control some of the more complex options using a mouse and keyboard to select them. One solution is the Elgato Stream Deck (£70-£220). This is a set of configurable hardware buttons that allow you to have numerous commands just a button push away. Available in 6, 15 and 32 key versions, the Stream Deck was originally targeted at gamers and streamers who wanted to switch sources, change lighting or play media clips easily.

Here's what my Stream Deck setup looks like - I keep this at arm's length, within reach, but just out of shot when presenting:

Figure 51: Stream Deck provides programmable buttons for shortcuts

Interaction

There are certain types of presentations where it's very desirable to get real time audience input in the form of a quick poll. For a confident presenter, this kind of dynamic interaction can really help to bring the presentation to life and offers the audience a sense of involvement and relevance rather than "Death by Slides".

Unbeknownst to many presenters, this sort of feature is actually built into PowerPoint and Google Slides but third-party services such as Sli.do and Poll Everywhere are alternatives offering some additional types of poll.

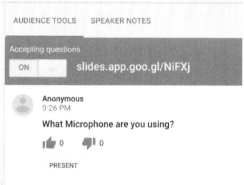

Figure 52: Google Slides includes the ability for attendees to ask questions that will be displayed to the presenter in Presenter View

Teleprompter

One of the reasons that a presenter in a professional venue or studio can appear so polished is that they often have a teleprompter device scrolling their speech for them to read, invisible to the viewers. This helps to eliminate the disfluencies that even the most experienced speaker can have when speaking to slides without a script. It also allows for full eye contact to maintain an audience connection.

Teleprompters use a specially coated sheet of glass known as a "beamsplitter" to display text on one side to the speaker while a camera can be on the other side and not see the text as it videos the presentation. The beamsplitter is typically at a 45-degree angle over the tablet and only the presenter sees the reflected text; the camera does not.

In the virtual world, some presenters may think that they can use a script as they aren't as visible to the audience - especially if they turn off their video after greeting the audience and then they can talk through their slides. Unfortunately, turning off your video disconnects you from your audience, and the temptation to read a script leads to monotonous delivery. It will also be obvious to your audience that you're reading if they can hear pages turning, so if you are going to do it, at least have your script on an iPad so you can swipe silently through the pages!

Software Teleprompters

There are a number of pseudo-teleprompter solutions that simply scroll your script for you in large letters on screen. If used in conjunction with a second monitor, this may be useful, but can encourage you to look at the text too much and not make eye contact with the camera/audience. If you don't have a "real" teleprompter, then I'm tempted to say don't use one at all—I personally find people staring off to the side really awkward as they read full sentences. But if you find it helps you present in a more fluid manner, then give it a go.

Software solutions include:
- https://www.easyprompter.com/
- https://cueprompter.com/
- https://teleprompter mirror.com/teleprompter software.htm

Tablet Teleprompters

The demand for ever increasing amounts of video content from vloggers and YouTube stars has led to a booming market for affordable teleprompter hardware. Unlike the physically large and expensive devices used in studios, this category of technology, once the sole preserve of professional studios and venues, is now seeing more widespread take up. Tablets have created an alternative market opportunity for low-end hardware devices to reflect a tablet (or even smartphone if you've good eyesight) screen into a functional teleprompter device. Although not comparable to the performance of a more professional setup with a 17" or 19" screen, a 10" tablet can power a semi-professional experience for presenters keen to maintain eye contact but in need of a script or reminders.

Figure 53: A tablet teleprompter costs from about £170 with a remote control; Camera/iPad not included

Teleprompter Tips

If you do use a teleprompter device, or just script-scrolling software, take extra time to prepare your script. Remember to write your script for speaking, not for reading. People don't speak in the same way they read and write, and the script can easily sound very stilted if not adapted for speech. Keep your sentences short, and use punctuation in the written script to remind yourself to pause when delivering it.

Using a teleprompter, it's even more important to back away from the camera/prompter even further than I advised earlier. The closer you are, the more obvious your eye movement will appear as you read. You'll need to experiment with the teleprompter font size settings to get the right balance of size - big enough to read at a distance, but small enough to get a meaningful number of words on the screen, or it won't be able to keep up with your pace. It's likely that the text on your prompter will be about 48 to 72 points in size. This means you will be able to fit about 5 words on each line. Ensure you scroll the text so that the line is read right in front of the lens, so it appears that you're looking right at the viewer. Remember, if it appears that you're looking other than straight ahead, you're not using the teleprompter effectively.

With a teleprompter of any kind, the speed at which it scrolls is of course crucial - it's vital to keep the text over the centre of the lens as you read it. Many teleprompters come with a remote control or in more sophisticated setups where you need your hands free, a foot pedal may be available, while the most sophisticated solutions use voice recognition, though this isn't helpful if you go off-script!

Multi-Source Media

A small number of presenters may want to go beyond what you can achieve with a single camera setup and, for example, be able to switch from a camera that shows them, to another camera that shows products, documents or a video feed of another source such as a gaming console. While your conferencing software likely does allow you to choose your video input, it's not always easy to switch sources during a presentation.

It is, though, surprisingly easy to achieve this kind of video mixing at home - you don't even always need any additional hardware, though hardware mixers are available from around £300.

Figure 54: Mini 4-input HDMI switchers are available from about £300

A popular software option for serious streamers is software called OBS (Open Broadcaster Software), available for free download. Combined with a keyboard shortcut or something more sophisticated like the Stream Deck device mentioned above, you can produce a complex presentation switching between cameras, web sites and slides seamlessly. Although a niche requirement, there may be growing interest for businesses to be able to create panel discussions in-house that look professionally-produced with multiple webcams in use.

Other Uses

If you do invest in some of the more advanced technology options, there are, of course, plenty of other ways to consider getting more usage out of them by moving your online presenting skills to other platforms - you could set up your own Podcast or YouTube channel or go commercial with Instagram or TikTok content.

Chapter 10: Summary

The aim for a good online presentation should be the confident delivery of quality content with the best possible production values. The content should be adapted and optimised for the online medium and special care should be taken to maximise the audio and video quality for the audience. In many cases, there's only a marginal gain from further investment in technology, especially once you've concentrated on and resolved the basics.

People will come from many different starting points in terms of their available technology, and their individual circumstances. Your decor choices were likely not made with full time broadcasting from your home as a priority. Regardless of whether you have the luxury of space which you can dedicate to creating a semi-professional area or whether you have to cobble together a temporary space, there's an encouraging combination of basic free tips and affordable technology supports that can make this stressful time less challenging, at least when it comes to presenting. And it's also less stressful to watch/attend a virtual event where the presenter has taken the time to review the basics and mitigate the most common and annoying distractions.

Maximum Impact: The Basics

I've included some more checklists in the Appendices but the top actions you can take to improve your online presentations are:

- Find your quiet space with a plain background
- Optimise your lighting
- Stand up and elevate your laptop/camera to eye level
- Move away from presenting *to* your laptop and start presenting *from* it; the laptop is your podium, not your audience
- Get the best microphone you can, close to your mouth
- Practice, Record and Review
- Slim down your content - visually and conceptually
- Know your tools - get confident navigating Zoom or the platform you're using
- Consider if there are any accessories that will make a real difference to your situation

Adapt and Thrive

When you're presenting from a stage or in an auditorium, you don't have to think about what people are seeing - you know immediately whether people can see your slides and your own position relative to the screen. Online, however, you need to be aware that different audience members may be looking at you differently. Your eyes and ears will deceive you - a scene that looks well-lit to you, may not look good on camera. You may sound fine as you listen to yourself, but your audience may be distracted by sounds you can't hear or have filtered out.

People have found themselves in all kinds of circumstances during the pandemic of 2020 and some have had an easier time adapting to remote working and online meetings than others. Regardless of whether you're fortunate to have been able to acquire an office for the garden, or requisition a spare room, or been forced to camp on the edge of a kitchen table between meals, there are things you can do to make the most of what is, for many people, a continually difficult situation.

Improvisation may be key - a simple stack of books to elevate a laptop can improve the sound, lighting and framing all in one fell swoop. Don't be afraid to improvise - that pile of books to prop up your laptop, or an extension cable may be one of the most liberating pieces of "technology"

Given the endless variety in presentations; presenters; and now presentation venues, there's no magic one-size-fits-all solution. But there are common guidelines that apply in almost all situations - focus on the content, practice the delivery and pick the right tools/technologies for your situation.

Environmental and furniture choices will influence your lighting, your sound, your camera framing, your ability to keep the things you need within reach and the likelihood of being interrupted. With fairly modest expenditure, you can almost certainly level-up your sound and video compared to the integrated hardware most people use. It's hard to imagine any presenter needing all of the technology described here - one person may benefit more from a £50 shield than a £200 microphone, while another may see the biggest payback from a £100 lamp.

Audience Appreciation

Your audience may not even notice the effort you've gone to. As I said earlier, thanks to the high expectations we have from TV, good sound and video isn't remarkable; only the lack of it is. However, it's less stressful to watch/attend a virtual event where the presenter has taken the time to review the basics and mitigate the most common annoyances. It lets the audience concentrate on the content, which I hope stands up to scrutiny too!

Remember too that not everyone's experience will be the same. What you think you look and sound like to your colleagues is probably not what they're seeing and hearing. With web-based meetings and meet-ups and professional online interaction becoming the stages for you to present yourself to your colleagues, how you look on your webcam and how you sound will be an increasingly important part of your professional image. Deliver that image wisely and it will pay off.

All Change

Understanding how to keep your audience engaged and working with the challenges of the medium and the technology require some strategic but necessary adjustments in the design and delivery of your online presentation. Ironically, presenting virtually can help some people who are nervous presenters, while unnerving people who are experienced in-person presenters, taking away the familiar environment and the audience they thrive on.

Please don't interpret any of the advice in this book as criticism of efforts to adapt to the new reality of virtual presenting - this guide is in no way intended to make anyone doing their best in these tough times feel inadequate - rather it aims to remove some of the pressures of presenting in this unfamiliar environment by pointing out pragmatic tips that offer quick wins as well as some guidance on choosing technological supports that may be unfamiliar and intimidating.

Although the bulk of this guide talks about the technology supports and considerations, that is what they should remain - secondary. Don't let worries about the novel challenges deflect you from your purpose - why you are presenting. It's not to look good or to prove that you do in fact have a better webcam than someone else. The focus must remain on your presentation goal - your pitch, your knowledge transfer, your message - delivered in the best way the channel allows, within your technical, personal, domestic and budget constraints.

Good Luck!

With preparation, improvisation and minimal budget, you can significantly improve the quality of your performance. Simple tips to make the most out of your environment, positioning and lighting can lift your image from messy to good. Targeted spend on upgrades appropriate to your situation can overcome challenges and make your presentation stand out. And if you want to go all out, there's an amazing range of top-quality accessories to put you on a par with broadcast quality productions, all from your home.

There's a range of technology issues that can undermine even the best presentation content in this new world, so take all the steps you can to maximise your technology and improve your technique, but content is still crucial. So remember, adapt your content for online viewing, stand up, raise the camera to eye-level, get the top of your head close to the top of the frame, light from the front and get the mic as close to your mouth as possible! Congratulations: you're presentation-ready!

Appendix 1: Checklists

Checklists are a great and simple tool to help ensure you don't forget any of the myriad things to check ahead of a presentation. You'll need to adapt these to your own circumstances, but hopefully they provide a basis to help ensure you don't forget something in the excitement of presenting (or the domestic chaos).

Setup & Preparation

- Laptop plugged in
- Any wireless devices fully charged (e.g. Bluetooth Microphone)
- Batteries for slide clicker
- Camera at eye level
- Microphone as close to you as possible
- Distracting background noises switched off (e.g. A.C.)
- Clock visible to you, ideally with timer
- Plenty of front-on lighting
- No deliveries scheduled or doorbell muted
- Phone on Do Not Disturb
- Glass of Water within reach
- Room well ventilated
- Housemates asked not to disturb or hog the Wi-Fi
- Plain or virtual background
- Fallback Plan considered (see Appendix 3)
- Communication channel established with Host
- Practiced Thoroughly
- Camera/Sound double checked
- Google/Alexa/Siri devices muted

Content & Delivery

- Start on Time!
- Succinct, highly visual content
- Interaction/Narrative Breaks planned to maintain engagement
- Look at the camera
- Smile
- Stand/Sit back from the camera

Appendix 2: Example Technology Choices

In this appendix, I've bundled some example techniques and products based on budget. At any price point there are often multiple excellent options but I want to illustrate the kind of product/feature ranges you might consider. Based on your own circumstances, you may want to over-invest in one area and ignore an another, but this is hopefully a useful starting point:

	Free/Low	Pragmatic	Polished	Pro
Lighting	Careful position	Lamp	External Light	Key Light(s)
Sound Accessories	Careful position	Pop Filter	Shock Mount	Boom Mount
Camera	Integrated (elevated)	C920	Kiyo	Brio
Microphone	Amazon Basics Desktop	Marantz	Yeti or SmartMike	Yeticaster or SmartMike
Background	None /Virtual	Virtual	Virtual	Green Screen
Approx. Budget	£40	£150	£500	£900

Prices typical at time of writing

Appendix 3: Fallbacks

Without trying to second guess everything that could go wrong to such an extent that it induces stress, it's sensible to prepare for the most likely technical challenges you may encounter. Having planned a little in advance can help turn a potentially stressful emergency situation into a smoothly navigated blip. It's particularly important to have a text message channel agreed with the host/organiser so you can contact them even if your laptop/Wi-Fi are offline.

Presentation Continuity Planning

Even if you've practised thoroughly, online presentations bring an added layer of complexity and risk of something going wrong. In fairness, the major platforms have coped amazingly well with the dramatic surge in demand due to the pandemic and have largely scaled up without incident or significant outages.

If you can, practice some scenarios in advance with colleagues and have a plan documented so that you'll be able to methodically work through a checklist (such as those below) rather than panic.

Software Issues

If Zoom, Microsoft Teams or Google Meet goes down centrally, then there's little you can do, and your audience will be similarly stuck. But if the software on your computer crashes, your audience may be left staring at a blank screen. In that event, the thing to do is to restart your computer and send a text message to the organiser/host to let them know you'll re-join momentarily. Also make sure:

- You don't have any other apps that auto-start up on your computer that could interfere with the presentation
- If you've made any setup changes - such as switching from your computer default webcam or microphone, know how to get to those settings quickly in case they don't persist after the reboot
- You have kept the link for the presentation session handy - keep it at the top of your inbox

- You know any password details required to re-join the session - don't get stuck without your Zoom login
- Remind the host to check you still have the required privileges e.g. screen sharing
- Make sure you have quick access to your slides - as understanding of an application crash as the audience may be, don't leave them waiting while you search for your slide deck

Connectivity Challenges

As I said in chapter 5, your internet connection is critical to your online experience. If you are encountering performance issues (for example if the audience tells you that your video is choppy), make sure your camera isn't set to too high a resolution/frame rate. Check you've set your presenting device to priority on the home Wi-Fi network, and make sure your housemates aren't streaming Netflix in 4K!

If your audience reports poor quality and you can't determine and resolve the issue quickly, then you could consider switching off video and seeing if it's possible to continue with voice only. Of course, that will negate a lot of the effort we've discussed in this book, but it may be a case of "the show must go on"!

If your broadband fails, again you need to notify the host via text. Then see if you can get it fixed in a reasonable time frame:

- Can you get to your router and reboot it?
- Do you know how to check for service outages on your provider's app or website via your phone?
- Will you suggest a postponement, can your host swap to another speaker or is it possible to run the session from your phone or a Wi-Fi Hotspot?

Mobile Backups

Although a computer with good broadband is the recommended minimum requirement, it may be possible in a tight situation to get by with a mobile connection, especially as 4G speeds improve and 5G begins to be more available and data allowances on mobile tariffs may be sufficient for a short video conference.

If your broadband fails you could try using a hotspot on your phone to re-join and keep going. Again, be prepared by making sure you know how to turn on your mobile hotspot and connect to it from your laptop.

As a final fallback, you may be able to make do with just your smartphone. With a headset, your sound should be ok, though depending on what phone and mic you have, you may be able to swap the mic to the phone in an emergency too. In advance, you'll need to ensure your smartphone has the Zoom app and you have a copy of your slides available on the device. You won't have any fancy virtual backgrounds but hopefully you'll be able to deliver the presentation even through adversity.

Acknowledgements

My thanks firstly to family, and to my friends who support my writing….especially Marie, Aideen, David, Caroline, Lorraine, Susan, Sylvia, Fergal, Lottie, Ken, Adam, Ian, Henning, Sinead, Louise, Matt, Sudha, Karolina, Paula, Orlagh, Pat, Luke, Trish and Rob, Roisin, Phelim, Caroline P, Claire and Eric, as well as Kevin, Lisa and Sabrina.

Also by the Author

Your Phone Can Save Your Life (2015)
Life as a Passenger (2017)
The New Acceleration (2018)
When Humans Stop Shopping (2020)

About the Author

David is an author and speaker specialising in the impacts of technology on society. He is a regular speaker on topics ranging from AI and Innovation in Business to Autonomous Vehicles, Technology in Healthcare and the Future of Retail.

As well as being a frequent guest lecturer at Stanford Continuing Studies, The Irish Management Institute and Technological University Dublin, David also works with select commercial clients including Mastercard, BMW and the Irish Academy of Computer Training.

For full colour versions of all the images in the book or to contact the author, visit the website at http://david-kerrigan.com/bop

Disclaimers

Although I use specific products as examples, I have no relationship with any of the vendors mentioned and always advise you to research the most suitable product(s) to meet your specific needs, which may vary from the scenarios I describe.

The screenshots of the various apps mentioned were all taken in November 2020 and are current as at that time. Inevitably, the software may change by the time you read this but the likelihood is that there will be even more features available to help you deliver great presentations online, so if you don't see the option I mention in the menu place I mention it, then root around to find it or its evolution.

Printed in Great Britain
by Amazon